LANDMARK DECISIONS OF THE UNITED STATES SUPREME COURT V

MAUREEN HARRISON & STEVE GILBERT
EDITORS

LANDMARK DECISIONS SERIES

EXCELLENT BOOKS
SAN DIEGO, CALIFORNIA

EXCELLENT BOOKS
Post Office Box 927105
San Diego, CA 92192-7105

Publisher's Cataloging in Publication Data

Landmark Decisions Of The United States Supreme Court V/
Maureen Harrison, Steve Gilbert, editors.
p. cm. - (Landmark Decisions Series)
Bibliography:p.
Includes Index.
1. United States. Supreme Court.
I. Title. II. Harrison, Maureen. III. Gilbert, Steve.
IV. Series: Landmark Decisions.
KF8742.H24 1991   LC 90-84578
347.'73'26-dc20
[347.30726]
ISBN 0-9628014-8-8

A Note To The Reader

Chiseled into the facade of the United States Supreme Court Building are these words:

EQUAL JUSTICE UNDER THE LAW

For many Americans, famous, infamous, and ordinary, the U.S. Supreme Court has been the last stop in their personal search for that elusive "equal justice under the law." This book, like its predecessors, is about some of those Americans. In the pages to follow you will find the extraordinary legal stories of kidnapped slaves, street corner preachers, a suspected traitor, an accused murderer, a convicted drug smuggler, a birth control advocate, a baseball player, women workers, an abused child, and a serial killer. People with little or nothing in common except that their personal search for equal justice led them one by one to the U.S. Supreme Court.

The Court has the final legal word on all Constitutional questions arising in the Federal Courts and all Federal questions arising in the State Courts. Since 1791 the Supreme Court has issued thousands of individual decisions. All have been important to the parties involved, but some, a significant few, have grown so important as to involve all Americans. These are Landmark Decisions, fundamentally altering the relationships of Americans to their institutions and to each other. Of these significant few, we have selected ten for inclusion in this book. These decisions represent the great and continuing debates and controversies of American history and politics. They are presented here in plain English for the first time to the general reader.

On the first Monday of each October the United States Supreme Court begins a new Term. From all over the country, on all kinds of issues, and for all kinds of reasons, Americans bring controversies to the Court for a final disposition. The Founding Fathers created the Supreme Court to construct and interpret the meaning of the Constitution. Chief Justice Charles Evans Hughes summed up the Court's responsibility in this way: "We are under a Constitution, but the Constitution is what the Judges say it is."

Every year over five thousand requests for review of lower court decisions are received by the Court. Requests, called *petitions for certiorari,* come to the Court from the losing side in Federal Appeals Courts or State Supreme Courts. Four of the nine Justices must agree to a review. Review is accepted in only four hundred cases each year. Once accepted, written arguments [briefs] pro and con are submitted to the Court by both the petitioner, the side appealing the lower court decision against them, and the respondent, the side defending the lower court decision in their favor. Interested parties, called *amici curiae,* friends of the court, may be permitted to file briefs in support of either side. After the briefs are submitted to and reviewed by the Justices, public oral arguments are heard by the Court in the Supreme Court chamber. Ordinarily the opposing sides, petitioner and respondent, are given thirty minutes of oral argument. The Justices, at their discretion, may interrupt at any time to require further explanations, to pose hypothetical questions, or make observations. Twice a week, on Wednesday and Friday, the Justices meet alone in conference to discuss each case and vote on its outcome. They may affirm [let stand] or reverse [change the outcome of], in whole or in part, the decisions of the lower courts from which these appeals have come. One Justice, voting in the majority, will be selected to write the majority opinion. Others may join in the majority opinion, write their own concurring opinion, write their own dissenting opinion, or join in another's concurrence or dissent. Drafts of the majority, concurring, and dissenting opinions circulate among the Justices, are redrafted, and recirculated, until a consensus is reached and a decision announced. It is the majority opinion as finally issued by the Court that stands as the law of the land. All other courts, Federal and State, are bound by Supreme Court precedent. The official legal texts of these decisions are published in the five hundred plus volumes of *United States Reports.*

Judge Learned Hand wrote: "The language of the law must not be foreign to the ears of those who are to obey it." The ten Landmark Decisions presented in this book are carefully edited versions of the official legal texts issued by the Supreme Court in *United States Reports.* We, as editors, have made every effort to replace esoteric legalese with plain English without damaging the original decisions. Edited out are long alpha numeric legal citations and wordy wrangles over points of procedure. Edited in are definitions (*writ of habeas corpus* = an order from a judge to bring a person to court), translations (*certiorari* = the decision of the Court to review a case), identifications (Appellant = William Marbury, Appellee = James Madison), and explanations (where the case originated, how it got to the court, and who all the parties involved were).

You will find in this book the majority opinion of the Court as expressed by the Justice chosen to speak for the Court. Preceding each edited decision, we note where the complete decision can be found. The bibliography provides a list of further reading on the cases and the Court. Also included for the reader's reference is a complete copy of the U.S. Constitution, to which every decision refers.

This is the fifth book in the **Landmark Decisions Series**. In each we have attempted to included an equal mix of history, controversy, and politics.

Landmark Decisions I includes School Desegregation, Obscenity, School Prayer, Fair Trials, Sexual Privacy, Censorship, Abortion, Affirmative Action, Book Banning, and Flag Burning.

Landmark Decisions II includes Slavery, Women's Suffrage, Japanese American Concentration Camps, Bible Reading In The Public Schools, A Book Banned In Boston, The Rights of the Accused, The Death Penalty, Homosexuality, Offensive Speech, and the Right To Die.

Landmark Decisions III includes Executive Privilege, Freedom of Speech, Forced Sterilization, Mob Justice, the Pledge of Allegiance, Illegal Search and Seizure, Interracial Marriage, Monkey Trials, Sexual Harassment in the Workplace, and Separation of Church and State.

Landmark Decisions IV includes Federal Supremacy, The Trail of Tears, Abraham Lincoln's Suspension of the Right of Habeas Corpus, Separate But Equal, Trust Busting, Child Labor, The Atomic Spies, Libel, Conscientious Objection, and Hate Crimes.

Chief Justice John Marshall wrote that a Supreme Court decision "comes home in its effects to every man's fireside; it passes on his property, his reputation, his life, his all." We entered into editing the **Landmark Decisions Series** because we, like you, and your family and friends, must obey, under penalty of law, the decisions of the U.S. Supreme Court. It stands to reason that, if we owe them our obedience, then we owe it to ourselves to know what they say, not second-hand, but for ourselves. We think it's time for you to have the final word.

M.H. & S.G.

TABLE OF CONTENTS

THE SLAVE SHIP CASES

That [the African slave trade] is contrary to the law of nature will scarcely be denied. That every man has a natural right to the fruits of his own labor is generally admitted; and that no other person can rightfully deprive him of those fruits, and appropriate them against his will, seems to be the necessary result of this admission.

Chief Justice John Marshall
The Antelope (1825)

They were native-born Africans . . . unlawfully kidnapped, and forcibly and wrongfully carried on board a vessel [the Amistad] which was unlawfully engaged in the slave-trade.

Justice Joseph Story
The Amistad (1840)

RELIGIOUS LIBERTY

The essential characteristic of [religious liberty] is that under their shield many types of life, character, opinion and belief can develop unmolested and unobstructed. Nowhere is this shield more necessary than in our country for a people composed of many races and of many creeds.

Justice Owen Roberts
Cantwell v. Connecticut (1940)

TREASON

The basic law of treason in this country was framed by men who were taught by experience and by history to fear abuse of the treason charge almost as much as they feared treason itself.

Justice Robert Jackson
Cramer v. United States (1945)

MILITARY JUSTICE
69

[W]e are not impressed by the fact that some other countries which do not have our Bill of Rights indulge in the practice of subjecting civilians who were once soldiers to trials by courts-martial instead of trials by civilian courts.

Justice Hugo Black
Toth v. Quarles (1955)

MARIJUANA
79

[Dr. Timothy Leary's] literal and full compliance with all the requirements of the [Marijuana Act] would have entailed a very substantial risk of self-incrimination.

Justice John Marshall Harlan
Leary v. United States (1969)

BIRTH CONTROL
103

[I]f the right of privacy means anything, it is the right of the individual, married or single, to be free from unwarranted government intrusion into matters so fundamentally affecting a person as the decision whether to bear or beget a child.

Justice William Brennan
Eisenstadt v. Baird (1972)

BASEBALL
117

Baseball has been the national pastime for over one hundred years and enjoys a unique place in our American heritage. . . . The game is on higher ground; it behooves every one to keep it there.

Justice Harry Blackmun
Flood v. Kuhn (1972)

This book is dedicated with love to our cousins

Sylvia Davidson

and

Rosie Cutler

THE SLAVE SHIP CASES

The Antelope

The Migration or Importation of such Persons as any of the States now existing shall think proper to admit, shall not be prohibited by the Congress prior to the Year one thousand eight hundred and eight.

The U.S. Constitution's Slave Trade Clause
Article 1, Section 9, Clause 1

The importation of African slaves into the United States was made illegal by the United States Congress commencing on January 1, 1808 after the expiration of the U.S. Constitution's Slave Trade Clause.

In 1819 the Antelope, a slave ship carrying over two hundred eighty kidnapped Africans, was captured by the U.S. Navy off the coast of Florida on suspicion of illegally smuggling African slaves. The history of her voyage is as follows: The Columbia, a slave ship, secretly sailed from Baltimore with an American crew. Off the coast of Africa she captured several Spanish and Portuguese slave ships. When Columbia was wrecked the crew and slaves were transferred to one of the captured ships, the Antelope, which sailed to the United States where she was captured.

The Spanish and Portuguese Governments claimed ownership of the Africans and demanded the immediate return of their property. The Africans appealed to the courts of the United States to be set free and returned to their homelands. After a hearing the Circuit Court of Georgia ordered the Africans returned to the Spanish and Portuguese. Counsel for the Africans appealed. The United States Supreme Court was asked to decide between the right of liberty and the right of property.

Chief Justice John Marshall delivered the opinion of the Court in March 1825. The edited text follows.

THE ANTELOPE COURT

Chief Justice John Marshall
Appointed by President John Adams
Served 1801 - 1835

Associate Justice Bushrod Washington
Appointed by President John Adams
Served 1798 - 1829

Associate Justice William Johnson
Appointed by President Jefferson
Served 1804 - 1834

Associate Justice Thomas Todd
Appointed by President Jefferson
Served 1807 - 1826

Associate Justice Gabriel Duvall
Appointed by President Madison
Served 1811 - 1835

Associate Justice Joseph Story
Appointed by President Madison
Served 1811 - 1845

Associate Justice Smith Thompson
Appointed by President Monroe
Served 1823 - 1843

The unedited text of *The Antelope* can be found on page 66, volume 23 of *United States Reports.*

THE ANTELOPE
MARCH 18, 1825

CHIEF JUSTICE MARSHALL: In prosecuting this appeal, the United States assert no property in themselves. They appear in the character of guardians, or next friends, of these Africans, who are brought, without any act of their own, into the bosom of our country, insist on their right to freedom, and submit their claim to the laws of the land, and to the tribunals of the nation. The consuls of Spain and Portugal, respectively, demand these Africans as slaves, who have, in the regular cause of legitimate commerce, been acquired as property, by the subjects of their respective sovereigns, and claim their restitution under the laws of the United States.

In examining claims of this momentous importance - claims in which the sacred rights of liberty and of property come in conflict with each other - which have drawn from the bar a degree of talent and of eloquence, worthy of the questions that have been discussed, this court must not yield to feelings which might seduce it from the path of duty, and must obey the mandate of the law.

That the course of opinion on the slave-trade should be unsettled, ought to excite no surprise. The Christian and civilized nations of the world, with whom we have most intercourse, have all been engaged in it. However abhorrent this traffic may be to a mind whose original feelings are not blunted by familiarity with the practice, it has been sanctioned, in modern times, by the laws of all nations who possess distant colonies, each of whom has engaged in it as a common commercial business, which no other could rightfully interrupt. It has claimed all the sanction which could be derived from long usage and general acquiescence. That trade could not be considered as contrary to the law of nations which was authorized and protected by the laws of all commercial nations; the right to carry on which was claimed by each, and allowed by each.

The course of unexamined opinion, which was founded on this inveterate usage, received its first check in America; and, as soon as these states acquired the right of self-government, the traffic was forbidden by most of them. In the beginning of this century, several humane and enlightened individuals of Great Britain devoted themselves to the cause of the Africans; and by frequent appeals to the nation, in which the enormity of this commerce was unveiled and exposed to the public eye, the general sentiment was at length roused against it, and the feelings of justice and humanity, regaining their long-lost ascendency, prevailed so far in the British parliament, as to obtain an act for its abolition. The utmost efforts of the British government, as well as of that of the United States, have since been assiduously employed in its suppression. It has been denounced by both, in terms of great severity, and those concerned in it are subjected to the heaviest penalties which law can inflict. In addition to these measures, operating on their own people, they have used all their influence to bring other nations into the same system, and to interdict this trade by the consent of all. Public sentiment has, in both countries, kept pace with the measures of government; and the opinion is extensively, if not universally, entertained, that this unnatural traffic ought to be suppressed. While its illegality is asserted by some governments, but not admitted by all; while the detestation in which it is held, is growing daily, and even those nations who tolerate it, in fact, almost disavow their own conduct, and rather connive at, than legalize, the acts of their subjects, is it not wonderful, that public feeling should march somewhat in advance of strict law, and that opposite opinions should be entertained on the precise cases in which our own laws may control and limit the practice of others. . . .

In the United States, different opinions have been entertained in the different circuits and districts; and the subject is now, for the first time, before this court. The question, whether the slave-trade is prohibited by the law of nations has been seriously propounded, and both the affirmative and negative of the proposition have been maintained with equal earnestness. That [the slave-trade] is contrary to the law of nature, will scarcely be denied. That every man has a natural right to the fruits of his own labor, is generally admitted; and that no other person can rightfully deprive him of those fruits, and appropriate them against his will, seems to be the necessary result of this admission. But from the earliest times, war has existed, and war confers rights in which all have acquiesced. Among the most enlightened nations of antiquity, one of these was, that the victor might enslave the vanquished. This, which was the usage of all, could not be pronounced repugnant to the law of nations, which is certainly to be tried by the test of general usage. That which has received the assent of all, must be the law of all. Slavery, then, has its origin in force; but as the world has agreed, that it is a legitimate result of force, the state of things which is thus produced by general consent, cannot be pronounced unlawful.

Throughout Christendom, this harsh rule has been exploded, and war is no longer considered, as giving a right to enslave captives. But this triumph of humanity has not been universal. The parties to the modern law of nations

do not propagate their principles by force, and Africa has
not yet adopted them. Throughout the whole extent of
that immense continent, so far as we know its history, it is
still the law of nations, that prisoners are slaves. Can
those who have themselves renounced this law, be permitted to participate in its effects, by purchasing the beings
who are its victims? Whatever might be the answer of a
moralist to this question, a jurist must search for its legal
solution, in those principles of action which are sanctioned by the usages, the national acts, and the general assent, of that portion of the world of which he considers
himself as a part, and to whose law the appeal is made. If
we resort to this standard, as the test of international law,
the question, as has already been observed, is decided in
favor of the legality of the trade. Both Europe and
America embarked in it; and for nearly two centuries, it
was carried on, without opposition, and without censure.
A jurist could not say, that a practice, thus supported, was
illegal, and that those engaged in it might be punished, either personally or by deprivation of property. In this
commerce thus sanctioned by universal assent, every nation had an equal right to engage. How is this right to be
lost? Each may renounce it for its own people; but can
this renunciation affect others?

No principle of general law is more universally acknowl-
edged, than the perfect equality of nations. Russia and
Geneva have equal rights. It results from this equality,
that no one can rightfully impose a rule on another. Each
legislates for itself, but its legislation can operate on itself
alone. A right, then, which is vested in all, by the consent
of all, can be divested only by consent; and this trade, in
which all have participated, must remain lawful to those
who cannot be induced to relinquish it. As no nation can
prescribe a rule for others, none can make a law of na-

tions; and this traffic remains lawful to those whose governments have not forbidden it. If it be consistent with the law of nations, it cannot in itself be piracy. It can be made so only by statute; and the obligation of the statute cannot transcend the legislative power of the state which may enact it.

If it be neither repugnant to the law of nations, nor piracy, it is almost superfluous to say, in this court, that the right of bringing in for adjudication [judgment], in time of peace, even where the vessel belongs to a nation which has prohibited the trade, cannot exist. The courts of no country execute the penal laws of another; and the course of the American government, on the subject of visitation and search, would decide any case in which that right had been exercised by an American cruiser, on the vessel of a foreign nation, not violating our municipal laws, against the captors. It follows, that a foreign vessel engaged in the African slave-trade, captured on the high seas, in time of peace, by an American cruiser, and brought in for adjudication, would be restored.

The general question being disposed of, it remains to examine the circumstances of the particular case. The *Antelope*, a vessel unquestionably belonging to Spanish subjects, was captured, while receiving a cargo of Africans, on the coast of Africa, by the *Arraganta*, a privateer which was manned in Baltimore, and is said to have been then under the flag of the Oriental republic. Some other vessels, said to be Portuguese, engaged in the same traffic, were previously plundered, and the slaves taken from them, as well as from another vessel then in the same port, were put on board the *Antelope*, of which vessel the *Arraganta* took possession, landed her crew, and put on board a prize-master and prize-crew. Both vessels proceeded to the coast of Brazil, where the *Arraganta* was wrecked, and her captain and crew either lost or made prisoners. The *Antelope*, . . . after an ineffectual attempt to sell the Africans on board, at Surinam, arrived off the coast of Florida, and was hovering on that coast, near that of the United States, for several days. Supposing her to be a pirate, or a vessel wishing to smuggle slaves into the United States, Captain Jackson, of the revenue-cutter *Dallas*, went in quest of her, and finding her laden with slaves, commanded by officers who were citizens of the United States, with a crew who spoke English, brought her in for adjudication. She was libelled [requested of the court] by the vice-consuls of Spain and Portugal, each of whom claim that portion of the slaves which were conjectured to belong to the subjects of their respective sovereigns; which claims are opposed by the United States, on behalf of the Africans.

In the argument, the question on whom the *onus probandi* [burden of proof] is imposed, has been considered as of great importance, and the testimony adduced [given] by the parties has been critically examined. It is contended, that the *Antelope*, having been wrongfully dispossessed of her slaves by American citizens, and being now, together with her cargo, in the power of the United States, ought to be restored, without further inquiry, to those out of whose possession she was thus wrongfully taken. No proof of property, it is said, ought to be required; possession is in such a case evidence of property. Conceding this as a general proposition, the counsel for the United States deny its application to this case. A distinction is taken between men, who are generally free, and goods, which are always property. Although, with respect to the last, possession may constitute the only proof of property which is demandable, something more is necessary where men are

claimed. Some proof should be exhibited, that the possession was legally. acquired. A distinction has been also
drawn between Africans unlawfully taken from the subjects of a foreign power, by persons acting under the authority of the United States, and Africans first captured
by a belligerent privateer, or by a pirate, and then brought
rightfully into the United States, under a reasonable ap-
prehension that a violation of their laws was intended.
Being rightfully in the possession of an American court,
that court, it is contended, must be governed by the laws
of its own country; and the condition of these Africans
must depend on the laws of the United States, not on the
laws of Spain and Portugal.

. . . . Whether . . . the *Antelope*, is to be considered as the
prize of a commissioned belligerent ship of war, unlawfully equipped in the United States, or as a pirate, it seems
proper to make some inquiry into the title of the claimants. In support of the Spanish claim, testimony is produced, showing the documents under which the *Antelope*
sailed from the Havana, on the voyage on which she was
captured; that she was owned by a Spanish house of trade
in that place; that she was employed in the business of
purchasing slaves, and had purchased and taken on board
a considerable number, when she was seized as prize by
the *Arraganta*. Whether, on this proof, Africans brought
into the United States, under the various circumstances
belonging to this case, ought to be restored or not, is a
question on which much difficulty has been felt. It is unnecessary to state the reasons in support of the affirmative or negative answer to it, because the court is divided
on it, and, consequently, no principle is settled. So much
of the decree of the circuit court as directs restitution to
the Spanish claimant, of the Africans found on board the

Antelope when she was captured by the *Arraganta*, is affirmed [confirmed].

. . . . We proceed next to consider the libel of the vice-consul of Portugal. It claims 130 slaves, or more, "all of whom, as the libellant is informed and believes," are the property of a subject or subjects of his Most Faithful Majesty; and although "the rightful owners of such slaves be not at this time individually and certainly known to the libellant, he hopes and expects soon to discover them." . . . These vessels were plundered in March 1820, and the libel was filed in August of the same year. From that time to this, a period of more than five years, no subject of the crown of Portugal has appeared to assert his title to this property, no individual has been designated as its probable owner. This inattention to a subject of so much real interest, this total disregard of a valuable property, is so contrary to the common course of human action, as to justify serious suspicion that the real owner dares not avow himself.

. . . . This long, and otherwise unaccountable, absence, of any Portuguese claimant, furnishes irresistible testimony, that no such claimant exists, and that the real owner belongs to some other nation, and feels the necessity of concealment.

. . . . These Africans still remain unclaimed by the owner, or by any person professing to know the owner. They are rightfully taken from American citizens, and placed in possession of the law. No property whatever in them is shown. It is said, that possession, in a case of this description, is equivalent to property. Could this be conceded, who had the possession? From whom were they taken by the *Arraganta*? It is not alleged, that they are the property of the crown, but of some individual. Who is that individual? No such person is shown to exist, and his existence, after such a lapse of time, cannot be presumed. The libel, which claims them for persons entirely unknown, alleges a state of things which is *prima facie* [at first glance] evidence of an intent to violate the laws of the United States, by the commission of an act which, according to those laws, entitles these men to freedom. Nothing whatever can interpose to arrest the course of the law, but the title of the real proprietor. No such title appears, and every presumption is against its existence.

We think, then, that all the Africans, now in possession of the marshal for the district of Georgia, and under the control of the circuit court of the United States for that district, which were brought in with the *Antelope*, . . . except those which may be designated as the property of the Spanish claimants, ought to be delivered up to the United States, to be disposed of according to law. So much of the sentence of the circuit court as is contrary to this opinion, is to be reversed, and the residue affirmed.

THE SLAVE SHIP CASES

The Amistad

At a slave auction held at Havana, Cuba in June 1839 two Cuban slaveholders, Jose Ruiz and and Pedro Montes, purchased fifty-two kidnapped Africans. One of those kidnapped Africans, captured several months before by Portuguese slavers on the northern borders of Sierra Leone, was a man named Cinque, ruler of the Kaw-Mendi tribe.

Ruiz and Montes, both Spanish subjects, herded their newly purchased slaves onto the slave ship Amistad, (Spanish for "Friendship") for transport from Havana to their Cuban plantation. The slaves, lead by Cinque, mutinied, killed most of their captors and spared others on the promise that those spared would sail the ship back to Africa. The Amistad was instead sailed by the surviving crew to the United States where, in August 1839, it was seized by the United States Navy off the coast of Long Island. The case of the murdered Spanish crew and the mutinous African slaves caused a public uproar. The Spanish Consul, on instruction from the Queen of Spain, demanded the return of the Africans, now called "pirates" and "murderers," under a 1795 Treaty with Spain. He wrote to President Van Buren: "[T]he Amistad [must] be immediately delivered, together with every article found on board at the time of her capture." The "Friends of the Amistad" hired ex-President John Quincy Adams to represent the kidnapped Africans. Adams replied to the Spanish claims that his clients were free, native-born Africans, kidnapped and unlawfully transported to the slave markets of Cuba in violation of that same 1795 Treaty. "Justice," Adams told the Court, " is felt and understood by all who understand human rights, is the constant and perpetual will to secure to everyone his own rights."

Justice Joseph Storey delivered the decision of the U.S. Supreme Court in January 1841. The edited text follows.

THE AMISTAD COURT

Chief Justice Roger Brooke Taney
Appointed by President Jackson
Served 1836 - 1864

Associate Justice Joseph Story
Appointed by President Madison
Served 1811 - 1845

Associate Justice Smith Thompson
Appointed by President Monroe
Served 1823 - 1843

Associate Justice John McLean
Appointed by President Jackson
Served 1829 - 1861

Associate Justice Henry Baldwin
Appointed by President Jackson
Served 1830 - 1844

Associate Justice James Wayne
Appointed by President Jackson
Served 1835 - 1867

Associate Justice Philip Barbour
Appointed by President Jackson
Served 1836 - 1841

Associate Justice John Catron
Appointed by President Jackson
Served 1837 - 1865

Associate Justice John McKinley
Appointed by President Jackson
Served 1837 - 1852

The unedited text of *The Amistad* can be found on page 518, volume 40 of *United States Reports.*

THE AMISTAD
JANUARY 1841

JUSTICE STORY: This is the case of an appeal from the decree of the circuit court of the district of Connecticut, sitting in admiralty [the navigable waters]. The leading facts . . . are as follows: On the 27th of June 1839, the schooner *Amistad*, being the property of Spanish subjects, cleared out from the port of Havana, in the island of Cuba, for Puerto Principe, in the same island. On board of the schooner were the master, Ramon Ferrer, and Jose Ruiz and Pedro Montez, all Spanish subjects. The former had with him a negro boy, named Antonio, claimed to be his slave. Jose Ruiz had with him forty-nine negroes, claimed by him as his slaves, and stated to be his property, in a certain pass or document, signed by the governor-general of Cuba. Pedro Montez had with him four other negroes, also claimed by him as his slaves, and stated to be his property, in a similar pass or document, also signed by the governor-general of Cuba. On the voyage, and before the arrival of the vessel at her port of destination, the negroes rose, killed the master, and took possession of her. On the 26th of August, the vessel was discovered by Lieutenant Gedney, of the United States brig *Washington*, at anchor on the high seas, at the distance of half a mile from the shore of Long Island. A part of the negroes were then on shore, at Culloden Point, Long Island; who were seized by Lieutenant Gedney, and brought on board. The vessel, with the negroes and other persons on board, was brought by Lieutenant Gedney into the district of Connecticut, and there libelled [requested of the court] for salvage [recovery of a ship or its cargo] in the district court of the United States. . . . On the 18th of September, Ruiz and Montez filed claims and libels, in which they asserted their ownership of the negroes as their slaves, and of certain parts of the cargo, and prayed that the same might be "delivered to them, or to the representatives of her Catholic Majesty, as might be most proper." On the 19th of September, the attorney of the United States for the district of Connecticut, filed an information or libel, setting forth, that the Spanish minister had officially presented to the proper department of the government of the United States, a claim for the restoration of the vessel, cargo and slaves, as the property of Spanish subjects, which had arrived within the jurisdictional limits [authority] of the United States, and were taken possession of by the said public armed brig of the United States, under such circumstances as made it the duty of the United States to cause the same to be restored to the true proprietors, pursuant to the treaty between the United States and Spain; and praying [asking] the court, on its being made legally to appear that the claim of the Spanish minister was well founded, to make such order for the disposal of the vessel, cargo and slaves, as would best enable the United States to comply with their treaty stipulations. But if it should appear, that the negroes were persons transported from Africa, in violation of the laws of the United States, and brought within the United States, contrary to the same laws; he then prayed the court to make such order for their removal to the coast of Africa, pursuant to the laws of the United States, as it should deem fit.

On the 19th of November . . . Antonio G. Vega, the vice-consul of Spain for the state of Connecticut, filed his libel, alleging that Antonio was a slave, the property of the representatives of Ramon Ferrer, and praying the court to cause him to be delivered to the said vice-consul, that he might be returned by him to his lawful owner in the island of Cuba.

On the 7th of January 1840, the negroes, Cinque and others, with the exception of Antonio, by their counsel, filed an answer, denying that they were slaves, or the property of Ruiz and Montez, or that the court could, under the constitution or laws of the United States, or under any treaty, exercise any jurisdiction over their persons, by reason of the premises; and praying that they might be dismissed. They specially set forth and insisted in this answer, that they were native-born Africans; born free, and still, of right, ought to be free and not slaves; that they were . . . unlawfully kidnapped, and forcibly and wrongfully carried on board [the *Amistad*], on the coast of Africa, which was unlawfully engaged in the slave-trade, and were unlawfully transported . . . to the island of Cuba, for the purpose of being there unlawfully sold as slaves; that Ruiz and Montez, well knowing the premises, made a pretended purchase of them; that afterwards, on or about the 28th of June 1839, Ruiz and Montez, confederating with Ferrer (master of the *Amistad*), caused them, without law or right, to be placed on board of the *Amistad*, to be transported to some place unknown to them, and there to be enslaved for life; that, on the voyage, they rose on the master, and took possession of the vessel, intending to return therewith to their native country, or to seek an asylum in some free state; and the vessel arrived, about the 26th of August 1839, off Montauk Point, near Long Island; a part of them were sent on shore, and were seized by Lieutenant Gedney, and carried on board; and all of them were afterwards brought by him into the district of Connecticut.

. . . . On the 23rd day of January 1840, the district court made a decree. By that decree, the court . . . allowed salvage to Lieutenant Gedney . . . , on the vessel and cargo, of one-third of the value thereof, but not on the negroes,

Cinque and others; . . . it dismissed the libels and claims of
Ruiz and Montez . . . as being included under the claim of
the Spanish minister; it allowed the claim of the Spanish
vice-consul, for Antonio, on behalf of Ferrer's representatives; . . . it rejected the claim made by the attorney of the
United States on behalf of the Spanish minister, for the
restoration of the negroes, under the treaty; but it de-
creed, that they should be delivered to the president of
the United States, to be transported to Africa, pursuant to
the act of 3d March 1819.

From this decree, the district-attorney, on behalf of the
United States, appealed to the circuit court, except so far
as related to the restoration of the slave Antonio. . . . No
appeal was interposed by Ruiz or Montez, nor on behalf
of the representatives of the owners of the *Amistad.* The
circuit court by a mere *pro forma* [for the sake of form]
decree, affirmed [confirmed] the decree of the district
court. . . . And from that decree, the present appeal has
been brought to this court.

The cause has been very elaborately argued . . . to dismiss
the appeal. On the part of the United States, it has been
contended:

> 1. That due and sufficient proof concerning the
> property has been made, to authorize the restitu-
> tion of the vessel, cargo and negroes to the Span-
> ish subjects on whose behalf they are claimed,
> pursuant to the treaty with Spain, of the 27th of
> October 1795.

> 2. That the United States had a right to intervene
> in the manner in which they have done, to obtain

a decree for the restitution of the property, upon
the application of the Spanish minister.

These propositions have been strenuously denied on the
other side. . . .

Before entering upon the discussion of the main points involved in this interesting and important controversy, it
may be necessary to say a few words as to the actual posture of the case as it now stands before us. In the first
place, then, the only parties now before the court on one
side, are the United States, intervening for the sole purpose of procuring restitution of the property, as Spanish
property, pursuant to the treaty, upon the grounds stated
by the other parties claiming the property in their respective libels. The United States do not assert any property
in themselves, nor any violation of their own rights, or
sovereignty or laws, by the acts complained of. They do
not insist that these negroes have been imported into the
United States, in contravention [violation] of our own
slave-trade acts. They do not seek to have these negroes
delivered up, for the purpose of being transferred to
Cuba, as pirates or robbers, or as fugitive criminals found
within our territories, who have been guilty of offences
against the laws of Spain. They do not assert that the seizure and bringing the vessel, and cargo and negroes, into
port, by Lieutenant Gedney, for the purpose of adjudication [judgment], is a tortious [wrongful] act. They simply
confine themselves to the right of the Spanish claimants
to the restitution of their property, upon the facts asserted
in their respective allegations [charges].

In the next place, the parties before the court, on the other side, as appellees [the parties appealed against], are
Lieutenant Gedney, on his libel for salvage, and the ne-

groes (Cinque and others), asserting themselves, in their answer, not to be slaves, but free native Africans, kidnapped in their own country, and illegally transported by force from that country; and now entitled to maintain their freedom.

. . . . The main controversy is, whether these negroes are the property of Ruiz and Montez, and ought to be delivered up; and to this, accordingly, we shall first direct our attention.

It has been argued on behalf of the United States, that the court are bound to deliver them up, according to the treaty of 1795, with Spain, which has in this particular been continued in full force, by the treaty of 1819, ratified in 1821. The sixth article of that treaty seems to have had, principally in view, cases where the property of the subjects of either state had been taken possession of within the territorial jurisdiction of the other, during war. The eighth article provides for cases where the shipping of the inhabitants of either state are forced, through stress of weather, pursuit of pirates or enemies, or any other urgent necessity, to seek shelter in the ports of the other. There may well be some doubt entertained, whether the present case, in its actual circumstances, falls within the purview of this article. But it does not seem necessary, for reasons hereafter stated, absolutely to decide it. The ninth article provides, "that all ships and merchandize, of what nature soever, which shall be rescued out of the hands of any pirates or robbers, on the high seas, shall be brought into some port of either state, and shall be delivered to the custody of the officers of that port, in order to be taken care of and restored, entire, to the true proprietor, as soon as due and sufficient proof shall be made concerning the property thereof." This is the article on which the main reliance is placed on behalf of the United States, for the restitution of these negroes. To bring the case within the article, it is essential to establish: 1st, That these negroes, under all the circumstances, fall within the description of merchandize, in the sense of the treaty. 2d, That there has been a rescue of them on the high seas, out of the hands of the pirates and robbers; which, in the present case, can only be, by showing that they themselves are pirates and robbers; and 3d, That Ruiz and Montez, the asserted proprietors, are the true proprietors, and have established their title by competent proof.

If these negroes were, at the time, lawfully held as slaves, under the laws of Spain, and recognised by those laws as property, capable of being lawfully bought and sold; we see no reason why they may not justly be deemed, within the intent of the treaty, to be included under the denomination of merchandize, and as such ought to be restored to the claimants; for upon that point the laws of Spain would seem to furnish the proper rule of interpretation. But admitting this, it is clear, in our opinion, that neither of the other essential facts and requisites has been established in proof; and the *onus probandi* [burden of proof] of both lies upon the claimants. . . . It is plain, beyond controversy, if we examine the evidence, that these negroes never were the lawful slaves of Ruiz or Montez, or of any other Spanish subjects. They are natives of Africa, and were kidnapped there, and were unlawfully transported to Cuba, in violation of the laws and treaties of Spain, and the most solemn edicts and declarations of that government. By those laws and treaties, and edicts, the African slave-trade is utterly abolished; the dealing in that trade is deemed a heinous crime; and the negroes thereby introduced into the dominions of Spain, are declared to be free. Ruiz and Montez are proved to have made the pretended purchase of these negroes, with a full knowledge of all the circumstances. And so cogent and irresistible is the evidence in this respect, that the district-attorney has admitted in open court, upon the record, that these negroes were native Africans, and recently imported into Cuba, as alleged in their answers to the libels in the case. The supposed proprietary interest of Ruiz and Montez is completely displaced, if we are at liberty to look at the evidence, or the admissions of the district-attorney.

If then, these negroes are not slaves, but are kidnapped Africans, who, by the laws of Spain itself, are entitled to their freedom, and were kidnapped and illegally carried to Cuba, and illegally detained and restrained on board the *Amistad*, there is no pretence to say, that they are pirates or robbers. We may lament the dreadful acts by which they asserted their liberty, and took possession of the *Amistad*, and endeavored to regain their native country; but they cannot be deemed pirates or robbers, in the sense of the law of nations, or the treaty with Spain, or the laws of Spain itself; at least, so far as those laws have been brought to our knowledge. Nor do the libels of Ruiz or Montez assert them to be such.

This posture of the facts would seem, of itself, to put an end to the whole inquiry. . . . But it is argued, on behalf of the United States, that the ship and cargo, and negroes, were duly documented as belonging to Spanish subjects, and this court have no right to look behind these documents; that full faith and credit is to be given to them; and that they are to be held conclusive evidence in this cause, even although it should be established by the most satisfactory proofs, that they have been obtained by the grossest frauds and impositions upon the constituted authorities of Spain. To this argument, we can, in no wise, assent. There is nothing in the treaty which justifies or sustains [upholds] the argument. We do not here meddle with the point, whether there has been any connivance in this illegal traffic, on the part of any of the colonial authorities or subordinate officers of Cuba; because, in our view, such an examination is unnecessary, and ought not to be pursued, unless it were indispensable to public justice. . . . What we proceed upon is this, that although public documents of the government, accompanying property found on board of the private ships of a foreign nation, certainly are to be deemed *prima facie* [on its face] evidence of the facts which they purport to state, yet they are always open to be impugned for fraud; and whether that fraud be in the original obtaining of these documents, or in the subsequent fraudulent and illegal use of them, when once it is satisfactorily established, it overthrows all their sanctity, and destroys them as proof. Fraud will vitiate any, even the most solemn, transactions; and an asserted title to property, founded upon it, is utterly void. The very language of the ninth article of the treaty of 1795, requires the proprietor to make due and sufficient proof of his property. And how can that proof be deemed either due or sufficient, which is but a connected and stained tissue of fraud? . . .

It is also a most important consideration, in the present case, which ought not to be lost sight of, that, supposing these African negroes not to be slaves, but kidnapped, and free negroes, the treaty with Spain cannot be obligatory upon them; and the United States are bound to respect their rights as much as those of Spanish subjects. The conflict of rights between the parties, under such circumstances, becomes, positive and inevitable, and must be decided upon the eternal principles of justice and international law. If the contest were about any goods on board of this ship, to which American citizens asserted a title, which was denied by the Spanish claimants, there could be no doubt of the right of such American citizens to litigate [bring to court] their claims before any competent American tribunal, notwithstanding the treaty with Spain. . . . [T]he doctrine must apply, where human life and human liberty are in issue, and constitute the very essence of the controversy. The treaty with Spain never could have intended to take away the equal rights of all foreigners, who should contest their claims before any of our courts, to equal justice; or to deprive such foreigners of the protection given them by other treaties, or by the general law of nations. . . . [T]here does not seem to us to be any ground for doubt, that these negroes ought to be deemed free; and that the Spanish treaty interposes no obstacle to the just assertion of their rights.

There is another consideration, growing out of this part of the case, which necessarily rises in judgment. It is observable, that the United States, in their original claim, filed it in the alternative, to have the negroes, if slaves and Spanish property, restored to the proprietors; or, if not slaves, but negroes who had been transported from Africa, in violation of the laws of the United States, and brought into the United States, contrary to the same laws, then the court to pass an order to enable the United States to remove such persons to the coast of Africa, to be delivered there to such agent as may be authorized to receive and provide for them. At a subsequent period, this last alternative claim was not insisted on, and another claim was interposed, omitting it; from which the conclusion naturally arises, that it was abandoned. The decree of the district court, however, contained an order for the delivery of the negroes to the United States, to be transported to the coast of Africa, under the act of the 3d of March 1819. The

United States do not now insist upon any affirmance of this part of the decree; and in our judgment, upon the admitted facts, there is no ground to assert, that the case comes within the purview of the act of 1819, or of any other of our prohibitory slave-trade acts. These negroes were never taken from Africa, or brought to the United States, in contravention of those acts. When the *Amistad* arrived, she was in possession of the negroes, asserting their freedom; and in no sense could they possibly intend to import themselves here, as slaves, or for sale as slaves. In this view of the matter, that part of the decree of the district court is unmaintainable, and must be reversed.

. . . . Upon the whole, our opinion is, that the decree of the circuit court, affirming that of the district court, ought to be affirmed, except so far as it directs the negroes to be delivered to the president, to be transported to Africa, in pursuance of the act of the 3d of March 1819; and as to this, it ought to be reversed: and that the said negroes be declared to be free, and be dismissed from the custody of the court, and go without [delay].

RELIGIOUS LIBERTY

Cantwell v. Connecticut

On April 26, 1938 Newton Cantwell and his sons, Jesse and Russell, all three ordained ministers of the Jehovah's Witnesses, were arrested on a residential street in New Haven, Connecticut while soliciting contributions and proselytizing individuals for their religious beliefs.

The Cantwells were charged with multiple violations of Connecticut's religious solicitation control law (they had not obtained the required municipal permission to solicit for religious causes) and with inciting others to breach the peace (some residents of the predominately Catholic street who were approached by the Cantwells were said to be so offended by the allegedly anti-Catholic nature of the solicitation that they were moved to threaten violence against the Cantwells). Father and sons were tried and convicted in a New Haven County Court of both soliciting religious contributions without prior municipal approval and inciting others to breach the peace by the the nature of their solicitation. The three Cantwells appealed for a reversal of their convictions to the Connecticut Supreme Court, asserting that Connecticut's religious solicitation control law, which they had all been convicted of violating, was itself in violation of the Due Process Clause of the Fourteenth Amendment and denied them the First Amendment guarantees of freedom of speech and free exercise of their religion. If this argument of unconstitutionality was accepted then the conviction of the Cantwells for incitement to breach the peace must also fall. Connecticut's Supreme Court rejected this argument and upheld their religious soliciting convictions. The Cantwells appealed to the United States Supreme Court.

Justice Owen Roberts delivered the unanimous opinion of the Court on May 20, 1940. The edited text follows.

THE CANTWELL COURT

Chief Justice Charles Evans Hughes
Appointed Chief Justice by President Hoover
Served 1930 - 1941

Associate Justice Pierce Butler
Appointed by President Harding
Served 1922 - 1939

Associate Justice James McReynolds
Appointed by President Wilson
Served 1914 - 1941

Associate Justice Harlan Fiske Stone
Appointed by President Coolidge
Served 1925 - 1946

Associate Justice Owen Roberts
Appointed by President Hoover
Served 1930 - 1945

Associate Justice Hugo Black
Appointed by President Franklin D. Roosevelt
Served 1937 - 1971

Associate Justice Stanley Reed
Appointed by President Franklin D. Roosevelt
Served 1938 - 1957

Associate Justice Felix Frankfurter
Appointed by President Franklin D. Roosevelt
Served 1939 - 1962

Associate Justice William O. Douglas
Appointed by President Franklin D. Roosevelt
Served 1939 - 1975

The unedited text of *Cantwell v. Connecticut* can be found on page 296, volume 310 of *United States Reports.*

CANTWELL v. CONNECTICUT
MAY 20, 1940

JUSTICE ROBERTS: Newton Cantwell and his two sons, Jesse and Russell, members of a group known as Jehovah's Witnesses, and claiming to be ordained ministers, were arrested in New Haven, Connecticut, and each was charged . . . in five counts, with statutory and common law offenses. After trial in the Court of Common Pleas of New Haven County each of them was convicted on the third count, which charged a violation of Section 6294 of the General Statutes of Connecticut, and on the fifth count, which charged commission of the common law offense of inciting a breach of the peace. On appeal to the [Connecticut] Supreme Court the conviction of all three on the third count was affirmed [upheld]. The conviction of Jesse Cantwell, on the fifth count, was also affirmed, but the conviction of Newton and Russell on that count was reversed and a new trial ordered as to them.

. . . [T]he appellants [the Cantwells] pressed the contention that the statute under which the third count was drawn was offensive to the due process clause of the Fourteenth Amendment because . . . it denied them freedom of speech and prohibited their free exercise of religion. In like manner they made the point that they could not be found guilty on the fifth count, without violation of the Amendment.

We have jurisdiction [authority] on appeal from the judgments on the third count. . . . Since the conviction on the fifth count was not based upon a statute, but presents a substantial question under the federal Constitution, we granted the writ of certiorari [agreed to hear the case] in respect of it.

The facts adduced [given] to sustain [uphold] the convictions on the third count follow. On the day of their arrest the [Cantwells] were engaged in going singly from house to house on Cassius Street in New Haven. They were individually equipped with a bag containing books and pamphlets on religious subjects, a portable phonograph and a set of records, each of which, when played, introduced, and was a description of, one of the books. Each [Cantwell] asked the person who responded to his call for permission to play one of the records. If permission was granted he asked the person to buy the book described and, upon refusal, he solicited such contribution towards the publication of the pamphlets as the listener was willing to make. If a contribution was received a pamphlet was delivered upon condition that it would be read.

Cassius Street is in a thickly populated neighborhood, where about ninety per cent of the residents are Roman Catholics. A phonograph record, describing a book entitled "Enemies," included an attack on the Catholic religion. None of the persons interviewed were members of Jehovah's Witnesses.

The statute under which the [Cantwells] were charged provides:

"No person shall solicit money, services, subscriptions or any valuable thing for any alleged religious, charitable or philanthropic cause, from other than a member of the organization for whose benefit such person is soliciting or within the county in which such person or organization is located unless such cause shall have been approved by the secretary of the public welfare council. Upon application of any person in behalf of such cause, the secretary shall determine whether such cause is a religious one or is a bona fide object of charity or philanthropy and conforms to reasonable standards of efficiency and integrity, and, if he shall so find, shall approve the same and issue to the authority in charge a certificate to that effect. Such certificate may be revoked at any time. Any person violating any provision of this section shall be fined not more than one hundred dollars or imprisoned not more than thirty days or both."

The [Cantwells] claimed that their activities were not within the statute but consisted only of distribution of books, pamphlets, and periodicals. The State Supreme Court construed [interpreted] the finding of the trial court to be that "in addition to the sale of the books and the distribution of the pamphlets the defendants [Cantwells] were also soliciting contributions or donations of money for an alleged religious cause, and thereby came within the purview of the statute." It overruled the contention that the Act, as applied to the [Cantwells], offends the due process clause of the Fourteenth Amendment, because it abridges or denies religious freedom and liberty of speech and press. The court stated that it was the solicitation that brought the [Cantwells] within the sweep of the Act and not their other activities in the dissemination of literature. It declared the legislation constitutional as an effort by the State to protect the public against fraud and imposition in the solicitation of funds for what purported to be religious, charitable, or philanthropic causes.

The facts which were held to support the conviction of Jesse Cantwell on the fifth count were that he stopped two men in the street, asked, and received, permission to play a phonograph record, and played the record "Enemies," which attacked the religion and church of the two men, who were Catholics. Both were incensed by the contents of the record and were tempted to strike Cantwell unless he went away. On being told to be on his way he left their presence. There was no evidence that he was personally offensive or entered into any argument with those he interviewed.

The court held that the charge was not assault or breach of the peace or threats on Cantwell's part, but invoking or inciting others to breach of the peace, and that the facts supported the conviction of that offense.

First. We hold that the statute, as construed and applied to the [Cantwells], deprives them of their liberty without due process of law in contravention [violation] of the Fourteenth Amendment. The fundamental concept of liberty embodied in that Amendment embraces the liberties guaranteed by the First Amendment. The First Amendment declares that Congress shall make no law respecting an establishment of religion or prohibiting the free exercise thereof. The Fourteenth Amendment has rendered the legislatures of the states as incompetent as Congress to enact such laws. The constitutional inhibition of legislation on the subject of religion has a double aspect. On the one hand, it forestalls compulsion by law of the acceptance of any creed or the practice of any form of worship. Freedom of conscience and freedom to adhere to such religious organization or form of worship as the individual may choose cannot be restricted by law. On the other hand, it safeguards the free exercise of the chosen form of religion. Thus the Amendment embraces two concepts - freedom to believe and freedom to act. The first is absolute but, in the nature of things, the second cannot be.

Conduct remains subject to regulation for the protection of society. The freedom to act must have appropriate definition to preserve the enforcement of that protection. In every case the power to regulate must be so exercised as not, in attaining a permissible end, unduly to infringe the protected freedom. No one would contest the proposition that a state may not, by statute, wholly deny the right to preach or to disseminate religious views. Plainly such a previous and absolute restraint would violate the terms of the guaranty. It is equally clear that a state may by general and nondiscriminatory legislation regulate the times, the places, and the manner of soliciting upon its streets, and of holding meetings thereon; and may in other respects safeguard the peace, good order and comfort of the community, without unconstitutionally invading the liberties protected by the Fourteenth Amendment. The [Cantwells] are right in their insistence that the Act in question is not such a regulation. If a certificate is procured, solicitation is permitted without restraint but, in the absence of a certificate, solicitation is altogether prohibited.

The [Cantwells] urge that to require them to obtain a certificate as a condition of soliciting support for their views amounts to a prior restraint on the exercise of their religion within the meaning of the Constitution. The State insists that the Act, as construed by the Supreme Court of Connecticut, imposes no previous restraint upon the dissemination of religious views or teaching but merely safeguards against the perpetration of frauds under the cloak of religion. Conceding that this is so, the question remains whether the method adopted by Connecticut to that end transgresses the liberty safeguarded by the Constitution.

The general regulation, in the public interest, of solicitation, which does not involve any religious test and does not unreasonably obstruct or delay the collection of funds, is not open to any constitutional objection, even though the collection be for a religious purpose. Such regulation would not constitute a prohibited previous restraint on the free exercise of religion or interpose an inadmissible obstacle to its exercise.

It will be noted, however, that the Act requires an application to the secretary of the public welfare council of the State; that he is empowered to determine whether the cause is a religious one, and that the issue of a certificate depends upon his affirmative action. If he finds that the cause is not that of religion, to solicit for it becomes a crime. He is not to issue a certificate as a matter of course. His decision to issue or refuse it involves appraisal of facts, the exercise of judgment, and the formation of an opinion. He is authorized to withhold his approval if he determines that the cause is not a religious one. Such a censorship of religion as the means of determining its right to survive is a denial of liberty protected by the First Amendment and included in the liberty which is within the protection of the Fourteenth.

The State asserts that if the licensing officer acts arbitrarily, capriciously, or corruptly, his action is subject to judicial correction. Counsel refer to the rule prevailing in Connecticut that the decision of a commission or an administrative official will be reviewed upon a claim that "it works material damage to individual or corporate rights, or invades or threatens such rights, or is so unreasonable as to justify judicial intervention, or is not consonant with justice, or that a legal duty has not been performed." It is suggested that the statute is to be read as requiring the officer to issue a certificate unless the cause in question is clearly not a religious one; and that if he violates his duty his action will be corrected by a court.

To this suggestion there are several sufficient answers. The line between a discretionary and a ministerial act is not always easy to mark and the statute has not been construed by the State court to impose a mere ministerial duty on the secretary of the welfare council. Upon his decision as to the nature of the cause, the right to solicit depends. Moreover, the availability of a judicial remedy for abuses in the system of licensing still leaves that system one of previous restraint which, in the field of free speech and press, we have held inadmissible. A statute authorizing previous restraint upon the exercise of the guaranteed freedom by judicial decision after trial is as obnoxious to the Constitution as one providing for like restraint by administrative action.

Nothing we have said is intended even remotely to imply that, under the cloak of religion, persons may, with impunity, commit frauds upon the public. Certainly penal laws are available to punish such conduct. Even the exercise of religion may be at some slight inconvenience in order that the state may protect its citizens from injury. Without doubt a state may protect its citizens from fraudulent solicitation by requiring a stranger in the community, before permitting him publicly to solicit funds for any purpose, to establish his identity and his authority to act for the cause which he purports to represent. The state is likewise free to regulate the time and manner of solicitation generally, in the interest of public safety, peace, comfort or convenience. But to condition the solicitation of aid for the perpetuation of religious views or systems upon a license, the grant of which rests in the exercise of a determination by state authority as to what is a religious cause, is to lay a forbidden burden upon the exercise of liberty protected by the Constitution.

Second. We hold that, in the circumstances disclosed, the conviction of Jesse Cantwell on the fifth count must be set aside. Decision as to the lawfulness of the conviction demands the weighing of two conflicting interests. The fundamental law declares the interest of the United States that the free exercise of religion be not prohibited and that freedom to communicate information and opinion be not abridged. The state of Connecticut has an obvious interest in the preservation and protection of peace and good order within her borders. We must determine whether the alleged protection of the State's interest, means to which end would, in the absence of limitation by the federal Constitution, lie wholly within the State's discretion, has been pressed, in this instance, to a point where it has come into fatal collision with the overriding interest protected by the federal compact.

Conviction on the fifth count was not pursuant to a statute evincing a legislative judgment that street discussion of religious affairs, because of its tendency to provoke disorder, should be regulated, or a judgment that the playing of a phonograph on the streets should in the interest of comfort or privacy be limited or prevented. Violation of an Act exhibiting such a legislative judgment and narrowly drawn to prevent the supposed evil, would pose a question differing from that we must here answer. Such a declaration of the State's policy would weigh heavily in any challenge of the law as infringing constitutional limitations. Here, however, the judgment is based on a common law [law based on judicial decisions] concept of the most general and undefined nature. The [lower court] has held that [Cantwell's] conduct constituted the commission of an offense under the State law, and we accept its decision as binding upon us to that extent.

The offense known as breach of the peace embraces a great variety of conduct destroying or menacing public order and tranquillity. It includes not only violent acts but acts and words likely to produce violence in others. No one would have the hardihood to suggest that the principle of freedom of speech sanctions incitement to riot or that religious liberty connotes the privilege to exhort others to physical attack upon those belonging to another sect. When clear and present danger of riot, disorder, interference with traffic upon the public streets, or other immediate threat to public safety, peace, or order, appears, the power of the state to prevent or punish is obvious. Equally obvious is it that a state may not unduly suppress free communication of views, religious or other, under the guise of conserving desirable conditions. Here we have a situation analogous to a conviction under a statute sweeping in a great variety of conduct under a general and indefinite characterization, and leaving to the executive and judicial branches too wide a discretion in its application.

Having these considerations in mind, we note that Jesse Cantwell, on April 26, 1938, was upon a public street, where he had a right to be, and where he had a right peacefully to impart his views to others. There is no showing that his deportment was noisy, truculent, overbearing or offensive. He requested of two pedestrians permission to play to them a phonograph record. The permission was granted. It is not claimed that he intended to insult or affront the hearers by playing the record. It is plain that he wished only to interest them in his propaganda. The sound of the phonograph is not shown to have disturbed residents of the street, to have drawn a crowd, or to have impeded traffic. Thus far he had invaded no right or interest of the public or of the men accosted.

The record played by Cantwell embodies a general attack on all organized religious systems as instruments of Satan and injurious to man; it then singles out the Roman Catholic Church for strictures couched in terms which naturally would offend not only persons of that persuasion, but all others who respect the honestly held religious faith of their fellows. The hearers were in fact highly offended. One of them said he felt like hitting Cantwell and the other that he was tempted to throw Cantwell off the street. The one who testified he felt like hitting Cantwell said, in answer to the question "Did you do anything else or have any other reaction?" "No, sir, because he said he would take the victrola and he went." The other witness testified that he told Cantwell he had better get off the street before something happened to him and that was the end of the matter as Cantwell picked up his books and walked up the street.

Cantwell's conduct, in the view of the [lower court], considered apart from the effect of his communication upon his hearers, did not amount to a breach of the peace. One may, however, be guilty of the offense if he commit acts or make statements likely to provoke violence and disturbance of good order, even though no such eventuality be intended. Decisions to this effect are many, but examination discloses that, in practically all, the provocative language which was held to amount to a breach of the peace consisted of profane, indecent, or abusive remarks directed to the person of the hearer. Resort to epithets or personal abuse is not in any proper sense communication of information or opinion safeguarded by the Constitution, and its punishment as a criminal act would raise no question under that instrument.

We find in [this] case no assault or threatening of bodily harm, no truculent bearing, no intentional discourtesy, no personal abuse. On the contrary, we find only an effort to persuade a willing listener to buy a book or to contribute money in the interest of what Cantwell, however misguided others may think him, conceived to be true religion.

In the realm of religious faith, and in that of political belief, sharp differences arise. In both fields the tenets of one man may seem the rankest error to his neighbor. To persuade others to his own point of view, the pleader, as we know, at times, resorts to exaggeration, to vilification of men who have been, or are, prominent in church or state, and even to false statement. But the people of this nation have ordained in the light of history, that, in spite of the probability of excesses and abuses, these liberties are, in the long view, essential to enlightened opinion and right conduct on the part of the citizens of a democracy.

The essential characteristic of these liberties is, that under their shield many types of life, character, opinion and belief can develop unmolested and unobstructed. Nowhere is this shield more necessary than in our own country for a people composed of many races and of many creeds. There are limits to the exercise of these liberties. The danger in these times from the coercive activities of those who in the delusion of racial or religious conceit would incite violence and breaches of the peace in order to deprive others of their equal right to the exercise of their liberties, is emphasized by events familiar to all. These and other transgressions of those limits the states appropriately may punish.

Although the contents of the record not unnaturally aroused animosity, we think that, in the absence of a statute narrowly drawn to define and punish specific conduct as constituting a clear and present danger to a substantial interest of the State, [Cantwell]'s communication, considered in the light of the constitutional guaranties, raised no such clear and present menace to public peace and order as to render him liable to conviction of the common law offense in question.

The judgment affirming the convictions on the third and fifth counts is reversed and the cause is remanded [returned to the lower court] for further proceedings not inconsistent with this opinion.

Reversed.

TREASON

Cramer v. United States

Treason against the United States shall consist only in levying war against them, or in adhering to their enemies, giving them aid and comfort. No person shall be convicted of treason unless on the testimony of two witnesses to the same overt act, or on confession in open court.

The U.S. Constitution's Treason Clause

Anthony Cramer immigrated from his native Germany to the United States in 1925 and became a naturalized U.S. citizen in 1936. In 1942 Cramer was living in New York City. On June 22 of that year Cramer was unexpectedly visited by two old friends calling themselves "William Thomas" and "Edward Kelly." Thomas and Kelly were in fact Wilhelm Thiel and Edward Kerling, English-speaking Nazi saboteurs sent to attack and destroy the U.S. defense effort. Thiel and Kerling had known Cramer from the time they had lived in the United States prior to the outbreak of war. They had been landed off the coast of Florida by a U-boat on the night of June 17 and were now hiding in New York City. Thiel and Kerling met with Cramer in a public place and without revealing their secret mission asked Cramer to hold a large amount of money for them. Cramer, while suspicious, agreed. The next day the F.B.I. arrested Cramer. He was charged with treason. Under the Constitution the crime of treason consists of two elements: adherence to the enemy and rendering that enemy aid and comfort.

Anthony Cramer was tried and convicted in U.S. District Court. The first American ever convicted of treason, his conviction was upheld by the U.S. Court of Appeals. Cramer appealed to the United States Supreme Court.

Justice Robert Jackson delivered the 5-4 opinion of the Court on April 23, 1945. The edited text follows.

THE CRAMER COURT

Chief Justice Harlan Fiske Stone
Appointed Associate Justice by President Coolidge
Appointed Chief Justice by President Franklin Roosevelt
Served 1925 - 1946

Associate Justice Owen Roberts
Appointed by President Hoover
Served 1930 - 1945

Associate Justice Hugo Black
Appointed by President Franklin D. Roosevelt
Served 1937 - 1971

Associate Justice Stanley Reed
Appointed by President Franklin D. Roosevelt
Served 1938 - 1957

Associate Justice Felix Frankfurter
Appointed by President Franklin D. Roosevelt
Served 1939 - 1962

Associate Justice William O. Douglas
Appointed by President Franklin D. Roosevelt
Served 1939 - 1975

Associate Justice Frank Murphy
Appointed by President Franklin D. Roosevelt
Served 1940 - 1949

Associate Justice Robert Jackson
Appointed by President Franklin D. Roosevelt
Served 1941 - 1954

Associate Justice Wiley Rutledge
Appointed by President Franklin D. Roosevelt
Served 1943 - 1949

The unedited text of *Cramer v. United States* can be found on page 1, volume 325 of *United States Reports.*

CRAMER v. UNITED STATES
APRIL 23, 1945

JUSTICE JACKSON: Anthony Cramer, the petitioner, stands convicted of violating section 1 of the Criminal Code, which provides: "Whoever, owing allegiance to the United States, levies war against them or adheres to their enemies, giving them aid and comfort within the United States or elsewhere, is guilty of treason."

Cramer owed allegiance to the United States. A German by birth, he had been a resident of the United States since 1925 and was naturalized in 1936. Prosecution resulted from his association with two of the German saboteurs who in June 1942 landed on our shores from enemy submarines to disrupt industry in the United States and whose cases we considered in *Ex parte Quirin.* One of those, spared from execution, appeared as a government witness on the trial of Cramer. He testified that Werner Thiel and Edward Kerling were members of that sabotage crew, detailed their plot, and described their preparations for its consummation.

Cramer was conscripted into and served in the German Army against the United States in 1918. After the war he came to this country, intending to remain permanently. So far as appears, he has been of good behavior, never before in trouble with the law. He was studious and intelligent, earning $45 a week for work in a boiler room and living accordingly.

There was no evidence, and the Government makes no claim, that he had foreknowledge that the saboteurs were coming to this country or that he came into association with them by prearrangement. Cramer, however, had known intimately the saboteur Werner Thiel while the latter lived in this country. They had worked together, roomed together, and jointly had ventured in a small and luckless delicatessen enterprise. Thiel early and frankly avowed adherence to the National Socialist movement in Germany; he foresaw the war and returned in 1941 for the purpose of helping Germany. Cramer did not do so. How much he sympathized with the doctrines of the Nazi Party is not clear. He became at one time, in Indiana, a member and officer of the Friends of New Germany, which was a predecessor of the Bund. However, he withdrew in 1935 before it became the Bund. He says there was some swindle about it that he did not like and also that he did not like their drilling and "radical activities." In 1936 he made a trip to Germany, attended the Olympic Games, and saw some of the Bundsmen from this country who went there at that time for conferences with Nazi Party officials. There is no suggestion that Cramer while there had any such associations. He does not appear to have been regarded as a person of that consequence. His friends and associates in this country were largely German. His social life in New York City, where he recently had lived, seems to have been centered around Kolping House, a German-Catholic recreational center.

Cramer retained a strong affection for his fatherland. He corresponded in German with his family and friends there. Before the United States entered the war he expressed strong sympathy with Germany in its conflict with other European powers. Before the attack upon Pearl Harbor, Cramer openly opposed participation by this country in the war against Germany. He refused to work on war materials. He expressed concern about being drafted into our army and "misused" for purposes of "world conquest." There is no proof, however, except for the matter charged in the indictment, of any act or utterance disloyal to this country after we entered the war.

Coming down to the time of the alleged treason, the main facts, as related on the witness stand by Cramer, are not seriously in dispute. He was living in New York and in response to a cryptic note left under his door, which did not mention Thiel, he went to the Grand Central Station. There Thiel appeared. Cramer had supposed that Thiel was in Germany, knowing that he had left the United States shortly before the war to go there. Together they went to public places and had some drinks. Cramer denies that Thiel revealed his mission of sabotage. Cramer said to Thiel that he must have come to America by submarine, but Thiel refused to confirm it, although his attitude increased Cramer's suspicion. Thiel promised to tell later how he came to this country. Thiel asked about a girl who was a mutual acquaintance and whom Thiel had engaged to marry previous to his going to Germany. Cramer knew where she was, and offered to and did write to her to come to New York, without disclosing in the letter that Thiel had arrived. Thiel said that he had in his possession about $3600, but did not disclose that it was provided by the German Government, saying only that one could get money in Germany if he had the right connections. Thiel owed Cramer an old debt of $200. He gave Cramer his money belt containing some $3600, from which Cramer was to be paid. Cramer agreed to and did place the rest in his own safe deposit box, except a sum which he kept in his room in case Thiel should want it quickly.

After the second of these meetings Thiel and Kerling, who was present briefly at one meeting, were arrested. Cramer's expectation of meeting Thiel later and of bringing him and his fiancee together was foiled. Shortly thereafter Cramer was arrested, tried, and found guilty. The trail judge at the time of sentencing said:

> "I shall not impose the maximum penalty of death. It does not appear that this defendant Cramer was aware that Thiel and Kerling were in possession of explosives or other means for destroying factories and property in the United Sates or planned to do that.

> "From the evidence it appears that Cramer had no more guilty knowledge of any subversive purposes on the part of Thiel or Kerling than a vague idea that they came here for the purpose of organizing pro-German propaganda and agitation. If there were any proof that they had confided in him what their real purposes were, or that he knew, or believed what they really were, I should not hesitate to impose the death penalty."

Cramer's case raises questions as to application of the Constitutional provision that "Treason against the United States shall consist only in levying War against them, or in adhering to their Enemies, giving them Aid and Comfort. No Person shall be convicted of Treason unless on the Testimony of two Witnesses to the same overt Act, or on Confession in open Court."

Cramer's contention may be well stated in words of Judge Learned Hand in *United States v. Robinson.*

> "Nevertheless a question may indeed be raised whether the prosecution may lay as an overt act a step taken in execution of the traitorous design,

innocent in itself, and getting its treasonable character only from some covert and undeclared intent. It is true that in prosecutions for conspiracy under our federal statute it is well settled that any step in performance of the conspiracy is enough, though it is innocent except for its relation to the agreement. I doubt very much whether that rule has any application to the case of treason, where the requirement affected the character of the pleading and proof, rather than accorded a season of repentance before the crime should be complete. Lord Reading in his charge in *Casement's Case* uses language which accords with my understanding: "'Overt acts are such acts as manifest a criminal intention and tend towards the accomplishment of the criminal object. They are acts by which the purpose is manifested and the means by which it is intended to be fulfilled.'"

The Government, however, contends for, and the [lower court] has affirmed [upheld], this conviction upon a contrary principle. It said "We believe in short that no more need be laid for an overt act of treason than for an overt act of conspiracy. . . . Hence we hold the overt acts relied on were sufficient to be submitted to the jury, even though they perhaps may have appeared as innocent on their face." A similar conclusion was reached in *United States v. Fricke*; it is: "An overt act in itself may be a perfectly innocent act standing by itself; it must be in some manner in furtherance of the crime."

As lower courts thus have taken conflicting positions, or, where the issue was less clearly drawn, have dealt with the problem ambiguously, we granted certiorari [agreed to

hear the case]. . . . Since our primary question here is the
meaning of the Constitutional provision, we turn to its solution before considering its application to the facts of
this case.

When our forefathers took up the task of forming an independent political organization for New World society,
no one of them appears to have doubted that to bring into
being a new government would originate a new allegiance
for its citizens and inhabitants. Nor were they reluctant to
punish as treason any genuine breach of allegiance, as every government time out of mind had done. The betrayal
of Washington by Arnold was fresh in mind. They were
far more awake to powerful enemies with designs on this
continent than some of the intervening generations have
been. England was entrenched in Canada to the north and
Spain had repossessed Florida to the south, and each had
been the scene of invasion of the Colonies; the King of
France had but lately been dispossessed in the Ohio Valley; Spain claimed the Mississippi Valley; and, except for
the seaboard, the settlements were surrounded by Indians -
not negligible as enemies themselves, and especially
threatening when allied to European foes. The proposed
national government could not for some years become
firmly seated in the tradition or in the habits of the people. There is no evidence that the forefathers intended to
withdraw the treason offense from use as an effective instrument of the new nation's security against treachery
that would aid external enemies.

The forefathers also had suffered from disloyalty. Success of the Revolution had been threatened by the adherence of a considerable part of the population to the King.
The Continental Congress adopted a resolution after a report by its "Committee on Spies" which in effect declared

that all persons residing within any colony owed allegiance to it, and that if any such persons adhered to the King of Great Britain, giving him aid and comfort, they were guilty of treason, and which urged the colonies to pass laws for punishment of such offenders "as shall be provably attainted of open deed." Many of the colonies complied, and a variety of laws, mostly modeled on English law, resulted. Some of the legislation in later years became so broad and loose as to make treason of mere utterance of opinion. Many a citizen in a time of unsettled and shifting loyalties was thus threatened under English law which made him guilty of treason if he adhered to the government of his colony and also under colonial law which made him guilty of treason if he adhered to his King. Not a few of these persons were subjected to confiscation of property or other harsh treatment by the Revolutionists under local laws; none, however, so far as appears, to capital punishment.

Before this revolutionary experience there were scattered treason prosecutions in the colonies usually not well reported. Some colonies had adopted treason statutes modeled on English legislation. But the earlier colonial experience seems to have been regarded as of a piece with that of England and appears not to have much influenced the framers in their dealings with the subject.

However, their experience with treason accusations had been many-sided. More than a few of them were descendants of those who had fled from measures against sedition and its ecclesiastic counterpart, heresy. Now the treason offense was under revision by a Convention whose members almost to a man had themselves been guilty of treason under any interpretation of British law. They not only had levied war against their King themselves, but they had conducted a lively exchange of aid and comfort with France, then England's ancient enemy. Every step in the great work of their lives from the first mild protests against kingly misrule to the final act of separation had been taken under the threat of treason charges. The Declaration of Independence may seem cryptic in denouncing George III "for transporting us beyond Seas to be tried for pretended offenses" but the specific grievance was recited by the Continental Congress nearly two years before in saying that " . . . it has lately been resolved in Parliament, that by force of a statute, made in the thirty-fifth year of the reign of King Henry the eighth, colonists may be transported to England, and tried there upon accusations for treasons, and misprisions [allowing a crime to happen], or concealments of treasons committed in the colonies; and by a late statute, such trials have been directed in cases therein mentioned."

The Convention numbered among its members men familiar with government in the Old World, and they looked back upon a long history of use and abuse of the treason charge. The English stream of thought concerning treasons began to flow in fairly definable channels in 1351 with the enactment of the great Treason Act. That was a monumental piece of legislation several times referred to in the deliberations of the Convention. It cut a benchmark by which the English-speaking world tested the level of its thought on the subject until our own abrupt departure from it in 1789, and after 600 years it still is the living law of treason in England. Roger Casement in 1917 forfeited his life for violating it. . . .

Adjudicated [decided] cases in English history generally have dealt with the offense of compassing the monarch's death; only eleven reported English cases antedating the

Constitution are cited as involving distinct charges of adherence to the King's enemies. . . . [T]he Act of Edward III did not contain the two-witnesses-to-the-same-overt act requirement which precipitates the issue here.

Historical materials are, therefore, of little help; necessity as well as desire taught a concept that differed from all historical models in the drafting of our treason clause. Treason statutes theretofore had been adapted to a society in which the state was personified by a king, on whose person were focused the allegiances and loyalties of the subject. When government was made representative of the whole body of the governed there was none to say "I am the State" and a concept of treason as compassing or imagining a ruler's death was no longer fitting. Nor can it be gainsaid that the revolutionary doctrine that the people have the right to alter or abolish their government relaxed the loyalty which governments theretofore had demanded - dangerously diluted it, as the ruling classes of Europe thought, for in their eyes the colonists not only committed treason, they exalted it. The idea that loyalty will ultimately be given to a government only so long as it deserves loyalty and that opposition to its abuses is not treason has made our government tolerant of opposition based on differences of opinion that in some parts of the world would have kept the hangman busy. But the basic law of treason in this country was framed by men who, as we have seen, were taught by experience and by history to fear abuse of the treason charge almost as much as they feared treason itself. The interplay in the Convention of their two fears accounts for the problem which faces us today.

We turn then to the proceedings of the Constitutional Convention of 1787 so far as we have record of them.

The plan presented by Pinckney evidently proposed only that Congress should have exclusive power to declare what should be treason and misprision of treason against the United States. The Committee on Detail, apparently not specifically instructed on the subject, reported a draft Constitution which left no such latitude to create new treasons. It provided that: "Treason against the United States shall consist only in levying war against the United States, or any of them; and in adhering to the enemies of the United States, or any of them. The Legislature of the United States shall have power to declare the punishment of treason. No person shall be convicted of treason, unless on the testimony of two witnesses. No attainder of treason shall work corruption of bloods, nor forfeiture, except during the life of the person attainted."

. . . . Distrust of treason prosecutions was not just a transient mood of the Revolutionists. In the century and a half of our national existence not one execution on a Federal treason conviction has taken place. Never before has this Court had occasion to review a conviction. In the few cases that have been prosecuted the treason clause has had its only judicial construction by individual Justices of this Court presiding at trials on circuit or by district or circuit judges. After constitutional requirements have been satisfied, and after juries have convicted and courts have sentenced, Presidents again and again have intervened to mitigate judicial severity or to pardon entirely. We have managed to do without treason prosecutions to a degree that probably would be impossible except while a people was singularly confident of external security and internal stability.

Historical materials aid interpretation chiefly in that they show two kinds of dangers against which the framers were concerned to guard the treason offense: (1) perversion by established authority to repress peaceful political opposition; and (2) conviction of the innocent as a result of perjury, passion, or inadequate evidence. The first danger could be diminished by closely circumscribing the kind of conduct which should be treason - making the constitutional definition exclusive, making it clear, and making the offense one not susceptible of being inferred from all sorts of insubordinations. The second danger lay in the manner of trial and was one which would be diminished mainly by procedural requirements - mainly but not wholly for the hazards of trial also would be diminished by confining the treason offense to kinds of conduct susceptible of reasonably sure proof. The concern uppermost in the framers' minds, that mere mental attitudes or expressions should not be treason, influenced both definition of the crime and procedure for its trial. In the proposed Constitution the first sentence of the treason article undertook to define the offense; the second, to surround its trial with procedural safeguards.

.... It is not easy, if indeed possible, to think of a way in which "aid and comfort" can be "given" to an enemy except by some kind of action. Its very nature partakes of a deed or physical activity as opposed to a mental operation.

Thus the crime of treason consists of two elements: adherence to the enemy; and rendering him aid and comfort. A citizen intellectually or emotionally may favor the enemy and harbor sympathies or convictions disloyal to this country's policy or interest, but so long as he commits no act of aid and comfort to the enemy, there is no treason. On the other hand, a citizen may take actions which do aid and comfort the enemy - making a speech critical of the government or opposing its measures, profiteering,

striking in defense plants or essential work, and the hundred other things which impair our cohesion and diminish
our strength - but if there is no adherence to the enemy in
this, if there is no intent to betray, there is no treason.

. . . . While to prove giving of aid and comfort would require the prosecution to show actions and deeds, if the
Constitution stopped there, such acts could be inferred
from circumstantial evidence. This the framers thought
would not do. So they added what in effect is a command
that the overt acts must be established by direct evidence,
and the direct testimony must be that of two witnesses
instead of one. In this sense the overt act procedural provision adds something, and something important, to the
definition.

Our problem begins where the Constitution ends. That instrument omits to specify what relation the indispensable
overt act must sustain to the two elements of the offense
as defined: adherence and giving aid and comfort. It requires that two witnesses testify to the same overt act, and
clearly enough the act must show something toward treason, but what? Must the act be one of giving aid and
comfort? If so, how must adherence to the enemy, the
disloyal state of mind, be shown?

[Cramer] especially challenges the sufficiency of the
overt acts to prove treasonable intention. . . . [T]o make
treason the defendant not only must intend the act, but he
must intend to betray his country by means of the act. It
is here that Cramer defends. The issue is joined between
conflicting theories as to how this treacherous intention
and treasonable purpose must be made to appear.

.... What is designed in the mind of an accused never is susceptible of proof by direct testimony. If we were to hold that the disloyal and treacherous intention must be proved by the direct testimony of two witnesses, it would be to hold that it is never provable. It seems obvious that adherence to the enemy, in the sense of a disloyal state of mind, cannot be, and is not required to be, proved by deposition [testimony] of two witnesses.

Since intent must be inferred from conduct of some sort, we think it is permissible to draw usual reasonable inferences as to intent from the overt acts. The law of treason, like the law of lesser crimes, assumes every man to intend the natural consequences which one standing in his circumstances and possessing his knowledge would reasonable expect to result from his acts. Proof that a citizen did give aid and comfort to an enemy may well be in the circumstances sufficient evidence that he adhered to that enemy and intended and purposed to strike at his own country. It may be doubted whether it would be what the founders intended, or whether it would well serve any of the ends they cherished, to hold the treason offense available to punish only those who make their treacherous intentions more evident than may be done by rendering aid and comfort to an enemy. Treason - insidious and dangerous treason - is the work of the shrewd and crafty more often than of the simple and impulsive.

While of course it must be proved that the accused acted with an intention and purpose to betray or there is no treason, we think that in some circumstances at least the overt act itself will be evidence of the treasonable purpose and intent. But that still leaves us with exceedingly difficult problems. How decisively must treacherous intention be made manifest in the act itself? Will a scintilla of evi-

dence of traitorous intent suffice? Or must it be sufficient to convince beyond reasonable doubt? Or need it
show only that treasonable intent was more probable than
not? Must the overt act be appraised for legal sufficiency
only as supported by the testimony of two witnesses, or
may other evidence be thrown into the scales to create inferences not otherwise reasonably to be drawn or to rein-
force those which might be drawn from the act itself?

It is only overt acts by the accused which the Constitution
explicitly requires to be proved by the testimony of two
witnesses. It does not make other common-law evidence
inadmissible nor deny its inherent powers of persuasion.
It does not forbid judging by the usual process by which
the significance of conduct often will be determined by
facts which are not acts. Actions of the accused are set in
time and place in many relationships. Environment illu-
minates the meaning of acts, as context does that of
words. What a man is up to may be clear from considering his bare acts by themselves; often it is made clear
when we know the reciprocity and sequence of his acts
with those of others, the interchange between him and
another, the give and take of the situation.

.... [I]t must be remembered that the constitutional provision establishes a minimum of proof of incriminating
acts, without which there can be no conviction, but it is
not otherwise a limitation on the evidence with which a
jury may be persuaded that it ought to convict. The Constitution does not exclude or set up standards to test evidence which will show the relevant acts of persons other
than the accused or their identity or enemy character or
other surrounding circumstances. Nor does it preclude
any proper evidence of non-incriminating facts about a

defendant, such for example as his nationality, naturalization, and residence.

. . . . It is obvious that the function we ascribe to the overt act is significant chiefly because it measures the two-witness rule protection to the accused and its handicap to the prosecution. If the overt act or acts must go all the way to make out the complete treason, the defendant is protected at all points by the two-witness requirement. If the act may be an insignificant one, then the constitutional safeguards are shrunken so as to be applicable only at a point where they are least needed.

The very minimum function that an overt act must perform in a treason prosecution is that it show sufficient action by the accused, in its setting, to sustain [uphold] a finding that the accused actually gave aid and comfort to the enemy. Every act, movement, deed, and word of the defendant charged to constitute treason must be supported by the testimony of two witnesses. The two-witness principle is to interdict [prohibit] imputation of *incriminating acts* to the accused by circumstantial evidence or by the testimony of a single witness. The prosecution cannot rely on evidence which does not meet the constitutional test for overt acts to create any inference that the accused did other acts or did something more than was shown in the overt act, in order to make a giving of aid and comfort to the enemy. The words of the Constitution were chosen, not to make it hard to prove merely routine and everyday acts, but to make the proof of acts that convict of treason as sure as trial processes may. When the prosecution's case is thus established, the Constitution does not prevent presentation of corroborative or cumulative evidence of any admissible character either to strengthen a direct case or to rebut the testimony or inferences on behalf of defendant. The Government is not prevented from making a strong case; it is denied a conviction on a weak one.

.... When we deal with acts that are trivial and commonplace and hence are doubtful as to whether they gave aid and comfort to the enemy, we are most put to it to find in other evidence a treacherous intent.

We proceed to consider the application of these principles to Cramer's case.

The indictment charged Cramer with adhering to the enemies of the United States, giving them aid and comfort, and set forth ten overt acts. The prosecution withdrew seven, and three were submitted to the jury. The overt acts which present the principal issue are alleged [charged] in the following language:

"1. Anthony Cramer, the defendant herein, on or about June 23, 1942, at the Southern District of New York and within the jurisdiction of this Court, did meet with Werner Thiel and Edward John Kerling, enemies of the United States, at the Twin Oaks Inn at Lexington Avenue and 44th Street, in the City and State of New York, and did confer, treat, and counsel with said Werner Thiel and Edward John Kerling for a period of time for the purpose of giving and with intent to give aid and comfort to said enemies, Werner Thiel and Edward John Kerling.

"2. Anthony Cramer, the defendant herein, on or about June 23, 1942, at the Southern District of New York and within the jurisdiction of this

Court, did accompany, confer, treat and counsel
with Werner Thiel, an enemy of the United
States, for a period of time at the Twin Oaks Inn
at Lexington Avenue and 44th Street, and at
Thompson's Cafeteria on 42d Street between
Lexington and Vanderbilt Avenues, both in the
City and State of New York, for the purpose of
giving and with intent to give aid and comfort to
said enemy, Werner Thiel."

. . . . It appeared upon the trial that at all times involved
in these acts Kerling and Thiel were under surveillance of
the Federal Bureau of Investigation. By direct testimony
of two or more agents it was established that Cramer met
Thiel and Kerling on the occasions and at the places
charged and that they drank together and engaged long
and earnestly in conversation. This is the sum of the
overt acts as established by the testimony of two witnesses. There is no two-witness proof of what they said nor in
what language they conversed. There is no showing that
Cramer gave them any information whatever of value to
their mission or indeed that he had any to give. No effort
at secrecy is shown, for they met in public places. Cramer
furnished them no shelter, nothing that can be called sus-
tenance or supplies, and there is no evidence that he gave
them encouragement or counsel, or even paid for their
drinks.

The Government recognizes the weakness of its proof of
aid and comfort, but on this score it urges: "Little imagination is required to perceive the advantage such meeting
would afford to enemy spies not yet detected. Even apart
from the psychological comfort which the meetings furnished Thiel and Kerling by way of social intercourse
with one who they were confident would not report them

to the authorities, as a loyal citizen should, the meetings
gave them a source of information and an avenue for contact. It enabled them to be seen in public with a citizen
above suspicion and thereby to be mingling normally with
the citizens of the country with which they were at war."
The difficulty with this argument is that the whole purpose of the constitutional provision is to make sure that
treason conviction shall rest on direct proof of two witnesses and not on even a little imagination. And without
the use of some imagination it is difficult to perceive any
advantage which this meeting afforded to Thiel and Kerling as enemies or how it strengthened Germany or weak-
ened the United States in any way whatever. It may be
true that the saboteurs were cultivating Cramer as a potential "source of information and an avenue for contact."
But there is no proof either by two witnesses or by even
one witness or by any circumstance that Cramer gave
them information or established any "contact" for them
with any person other than an attempt to bring about a
rendezvous between Thiel and a girl, or that being "seen
in public with a citizen above suspicion" was of any assistance to the enemy. Meeting with Cramer in public drinking places to tipple and trifle was no part of the saboteurs' mission and did not advance it. It may well have
been a digression which jeopardized its success.

The shortcomings of the overt act submitted are emphasized by contrast with others which the indictment
charged but which the prosecution withdrew for admitted
insufficiency of proof. It appears that Cramer took from
Thiel for safekeeping a money belt containing about
$3,600, some $160 of which he held in his room concealed
in books for Thiel's use as needed. An old indebtedness
of Thiel to Cramer of $200 was paid from the fund, and
the rest Cramer put in his safe-deposit box in a bank for

safekeeping. All of this was at Thiel's request. That Thiel would be aided by having the security of a safe-deposit box for his funds, plus availability of smaller amounts, and by being relieved of the risks of carrying large sums on his person - without disclosing his presence or identity to a bank - seems obvious. The inference of intent from such act is also very different from the intent manifest by drinking and talking together. Taking what must have seemed a large sum of money for safekeeping is not a usual amenity of social intercourse. That such responsibilities are undertaken and such trust bestowed without the scratch of a pen to show it, implies some degree of mutuality and concert from which a jury could say that aid and comfort was given and was intended. If these acts had been submitted as overt acts of treason, and we were now required to decide whether they had been established as required, we would have a quite different case. We would then have to decide whether statements on the witness stand by the defendant are either "confession in open court" or may be counted as the testimony of one of the required two witnesses to make out otherwise insufficiently proved "overt acts." But this transaction was not proven as the Government evidently hoped to do when the indictment was obtained. The overt acts based on it were expressly withdrawn from the jury, and Cramer has not been convicted of treason on account of such acts. We cannot sustain a conviction for the acts submitted on the theory that, even if insufficient, some unsubmitted ones may be resorted to as proof of treason. Evidence of the money transaction serves only to show how much went out of the case when it was withdrawn.

The Government contends that outside of the overt acts, and by lesser degree of proof, it has shown a treasonable intent on Cramer's part in meeting and talking with Thiel and Kerling. But if it showed him disposed to betray, and showed that he had opportunity to do so, it still has not proved in the manner required that he did any acts submitted to the jury as a basis for conviction which had the effect of betraying by giving aid and comfort. To take the intent for the deed would carry us back to constructive treasons.

It is outside of the commonplace overt acts as proved that we must find all that convicts or convinces either that Cramer gave aid and comfort or that he had a traitorous intention. The prosecution relied chiefly upon the testimony of Norma Kopp, the fiancee of Thiel, as to incriminating statements made by Cramer to her, upon admissions made by Cramer after his arrest to agents of the Federal Bureau of Investigation, upon letters and documents found on search of his room by permission after his arrest, and upon testimony that Cramer had curtly refused to buy Government bonds. . . .

Most damaging is the testimony of Norma Kopp, a friend of Cramer's and one with whom, if she is to be believed, he had been most indiscreetly confidential. Her testimony went considerably beyond that of the agents of the Federal Bureau of Investigation as to admissions of guilty knowledge of Thiel's hostile mission and of Cramer's sympathy with it. To the extent that his conviction rests upon such evidence, and it does to an unknown but considerable extent, it rests upon the uncorroborated testimony of one witness not without strong emotional interest in the drama of which Cramer's trial was a part. Other evidence relates statements by Cramer before the United States was at war with Germany. At the time they were uttered, however, they were not treasonable. To use prewar expressions of opposition to entering a war to convict of treason during the war is a dangerous procedure at best. The same may be said about the inference of disloyal attitude created by showing that he refused to buy bonds and closed the door in the salesman's face. Another class of evidence consists of admissions to agents of the Federal Bureau of Investigation. They are, of course, not "confessions in open court." The Government does not contend and could not well contend that admissions made out of court, if otherwise admissible, can supply a deficiency in proof of the overt act itself.

The Government has urged that our initial interpretation of the treason clause should be less exacting, lest treason be too hard to prove and the Government disabled from adequately combating the techniques of modern warfare. But the treason offense is not the only nor can it well serve as the principal legal weapon to vindicate our national cohesion and security. In debating this provision, Rufus King observed to the [Constitutional] Convention that the "controversy relating to Treason might be of less magnitude than was supposed; as the legislature might punish capitally under other names than Treason." His statement holds good today. Of course we do not intimate that Congress could dispense with the two-witness rule merely by giving the same offense another name. But the power of Congress is in no way limited to enact prohibitions of specified acts thought detrimental to our wartime safety. The loyal and the disloyal alike may be forbidden to do acts which place our security in peril, and the trial thereof may be focused upon defendant's specific intent to do those particular acts thus eliminating the accusation of treachery and of general intent to betray which have such passion-rousing potentialities. Congress repeatedly has enacted prohibitions of specific acts thought to endanger our security and the practice of foreign nations with defense problems more acute than our own affords examples of others.

The framers' effort to compress into two sentences the law of one of the most intricate of crimes gives a superficial appearance of clarity and simplicity which proves illusory when it is put to practical application. There are few subjects on which the temptation to utter abstract interpretative generalizations is greater or on which they are more to be distrusted. The little clause is packed with controversy and difficulty. The offense is one of subtlety, and it is easy to demonstrate lack of logic in almost any interpretation by hypothetical cases, to which real treasons rarely will conform. The protection of the two-witness requirement, limited as it is to overt acts, may be wholly unrelated to the real controversial factors in a case. We would be understood as speaking only in the light of the facts and of the issues raised in the case under consideration, although that leaves many undetermined grounds of dispute which, after the method of the common law, we may defer until they are presented by facts which may throw greater light on their significance. Although nothing in the conduct of Cramer's trial evokes it, a repetition of Chief Justice Marshall's warning can never be untimely:

> "As there is no crime which can more excite and agitate the passions of men than treason, no charge demands more from the tribunal before which it is made, a deliberate and temperate inquiry. Whether this inquiry be directed to the fact or to the law, none can be more solemn, none more important to the citizen or to the government; none can more affect the safety of both. . . . It is, therefore, more safe as well as

more consonant to the principles of our constitution, that the crime of treason should not be extended by construction to doubtful cases; and that crimes not clearly within the constitutional definition, should receive such punishment as the legislature in its wisdom may provide."

It is not difficult to find grounds upon which to quarrel with this Constitutional provision. Perhaps the framers placed rather more reliance on direct testimony than modern researches in psychology warrant. Or it may be considered that such a quantitative measure of proof, such a mechanical calibration of evidence is a crude device at best or that its protection of innocence is too fortuitous to warrant so unselective an obstacle to conviction. Certainly the treason rule, whether wisely or not, is severely restrictive. It must be remembered, however, that the Constitutional Convention was warned by James Wilson that "Treason may sometimes be practiced in such a manner, as to render proof extremely difficult - as in a traitorous correspondence with an Enemy." The provision was adopted not merely in spite of the difficulties it put in the way of prosecution but because of them. And it was not by whim or by accident, but because one of the most venerated of that venerated group considered that "prosecutions for treason were generally virulent." Time has not made the accusation of treachery less poisonous, nor the task of judging one charged with betraying the country, including his triers, less susceptible to the influence of suspicion and rancor. The innovations made by the forefathers in the law of treason were conceived in a faith such as Paine put in the maxim that "He that would make his own liberty secure must guard even his enemy from oppression; for if he violates this duty he establishes

a precedent that will reach himself." We still put trust in
it.

We hold that overt acts 1 and 2 are insufficient as proved
to support the judgment of conviction, which accordingly
is reversed.

MILITARY JUSTICE

Toth v. Quarles

Any person charged with having committed an offense, while subject to the Code of Military Justice, punishable by confinement of five years or more and for which the person cannot be tried in the Courts of the United States, shall not be relieved from liability to trial by courts-marshall by reason of the termination of military service.

Article 3, The Military Code of Justice

Robert Toth, an ex-U.S. serviceman, was arrested in May 1953 in Pittsburgh, Pennsylvania by military authorities. Removed from the United States, Toth was to be tried by a military court for the murder of a foreign national allegedly committed while Toth had still been on active duty. Toth, now a civilian, honorably discharged from the Air Force 5 months earlier, was to be tried by a military court under Article 3 of the Military Code of Justice.

Enacted by the United States Congress in 1950 Article 3 of the Military Code of Justice had extended, in certain circumstances, the military's legal jurisdiction to all ex-U.S. servicemen. The legal rights - including the right to a trial by a jury of their peers - of over three million veterans of United States military service were effected.

Toth's sister Audrey filed a petition with the U.S. District Court for the District of Columbia demanding U.S. Air Force Secretary Donald Quarles release her brother from military custody. The District Court ordered Toth's release. The Air Force appealed to the U.S. Court of Appeals for the District of Columbia which reversed the judgement of the District Court. Toth, alleging Article 3 of the Code of Military Justice was unconstitutional, appealed to the United States Supreme Court.

Justice Hugo Black delivered the 6-3 opinion of the Court on November 7, 1955. The edited text follows.

THE TOTH COURT

Chief Justice Earl Warren
Appointed Chief Justice by President Eisenhower
Served 1953 - 1969

Associate Justice Hugo Black
Appointed by President Franklin D. Roosevelt
Served 1937 - 1971

Associate Justice Stanley Reed
Appointed by President Franklin D. Roosevelt
Served 1938 - 1957

Associate Justice Felix Frankfurter
Appointed by President Franklin D. Roosevelt
Served 1939 - 1962

Associate Justice William O. Douglas
Appointed by President Franklin D. Roosevelt
Served 1939 - 1975

Associate Justice Robert Jackson
Appointed by President Franklin D. Roosevelt
Served 1941 - 1954

Associate Justice Harold Burton
Appointed by President Truman
Served 1945 - 1958

Associate Justice Tom Clark
Appointed by President Truman
Served 1949 - 1967

Associate Justice Sherman Minton
Appointed by President Truman
Served 1949 - 1956

The unedited text of *Toth v. Quarles* can be found on page 11, volume 350 of *United States Reports*.

TOTH v. QUARLES
NOVEMBER 7, 1955

JUSTICE BLACK: After serving with the United States
Air Force in Korea, Robert W. Toth was honorably discharged. He returned to his home in Pittsburgh and went
to work in a steel plant. Five months later he was arrested by military authorities on charges of murder and conspiracy to commit murder while an airman in Korea. At
the time of arrest he had no relationship of any kind with
the military. He was taken to Korea to stand trial before
a court-martial under authority of a 1950 Act of Congress. The Court of Appeals sustained [upheld] the Act,
rejecting the contention that civilian ex-servicemen like
Toth could not constitutionally be subjected to trial by
court-martial. We granted certiorari [agreed to hear the
case] to pass upon this important constitutional question.

The 1950 Act cannot be sustained on the constitutional
power of Congress "To raise and support Armies," "To declare War," or to punish "Offenses against the Law of Nations." And this assertion of military authority over civilians cannot rest on the President's power as commander-
in-chief, or on any theory of martial law. The Government's contention is that the Act is a valid exercise of the
power granted Congress in Article 1 of the Constitution
"To make Rules for the Government and Regulation of
the land and naval Forces," as supplemented by the Necessary and Proper Clause.

This Court has held that the Article 1 clause just quoted
authorizes Congress to subject persons actually in the
armed service to trial by court-martial for military and
naval offenses. Later it was held that court-martial jurisdiction could be exerted over a dishonorably discharged

soldier then a military prisoner serving a sentence imposed by a prior court-martial. It has never been intimated by this Court, however, that Article 1 military jurisdiction could be extended to civilian ex-soldiers who had severed all relationship with the military and its institutions. To allow this extension of military authority would require an extremely broad construction of the language used in the constitutional provision relied on. For given its natural meaning, the power granted Congress "To make Rules" to regulate "the land and naval Forces" would seem to restrict court-martial jurisdiction to persons who are actually members or part of the armed forces. There is a compelling reason for construing [interpreting] the clause this way: any expansion of court-martial jurisdiction like that in the 1950 Act necessarily encroaches on the jurisdiction of federal courts set up under Article 3 of the Constitution where persons on trial are surrounded with more constitutional safeguards than in military tribunals.

Article 3 provides for the establishment of a court system as one of the separate but coordinate branches of the National Government. It is the primary, indeed the sole business of these courts to try cases and controversies between individuals and between individuals and the Government. This includes trial of criminal cases. These courts are presided over by judges appointed for life, subject only to removal by impeachment. Their compensation cannot be diminished during their continuance in office. The provisions of Article 3 were designed to give judges maximum freedom from possible coercion or influence by the executive or legislative branches of the Government. But the Constitution and the Amendments in the Bill of Rights show that the Founders were not satisfied with leaving determination of guilt or innocence to judges, even though wholly independent. They further provided that no person should be held to answer in those courts for capital or other infamous crimes unless on the presentment [accusation] or indictment [charge] of a grand jury drawn from the body of the people. Other safeguards designed to protect defendants against oppressive governmental practices were included. One of these was considered so important to liberty of the individual that it appears in two parts of the Constitution. Article 3, Section 2, commands that the "Trial of all Crimes, except in Cases of Impeachment, shall be by Jury; and such Trial shall be held in the State where the said Crimes shall have been committed; but when not committed within any State, the Trial shall be at such Place or Places as the Congress may by Law have directed." And the Sixth Amendment provides that "In all criminal prosecutions, the accused shall enjoy the right to a speedy and public trial, by an impartial jury of the state and district wherein the crime shall have been committed. . . ." This right of trial by jury ranks very high in our catalogue of constitutional safeguards.

We find nothing in the history or constitutional treatment of military tribunals which entitles them to rank along with Article 3 courts as adjudicators of the guilt or innocence of people charged with offenses for which they can be deprived of their life, liberty or property. Unlike courts, it is the primary business of armies and navies to fight or be ready to fight wars should the occasion arise. But trial of soldiers to maintain discipline is merely incidental to an army's primary fighting function. To the extent that those responsible for performance of this primary function are diverted from it by the necessity of trying cases, the basic fighting purpose of armies is not served. And conceding to military personnel that high degree of honesty and sense of justice which nearly all of them undoubtedly have, it still remains true that military tribunals have not been and probably never can be constituted in such way that they can have the same kind of qualifications that the Constitution has deemed essential to fair trials of civilians in federal courts. For instance, the Constitution does not provide life tenure for those performing judicial functions in military trials. They are appointed by military commanders and may be removed at will. Nor does the Constitution protect their salaries as it does judicial salaries. Strides have been made toward making courts-martial less subject to the will of the executive department which appoints, supervises and ultimately controls them. But from the very nature of things, courts have more independence in passing on the life and liberty of people than do military tribunals.

Moreover, there is a great difference between trial by jury and trial by selected members of the military forces. It is true that military personnel because of their training and experience may be especially competent to try soldiers for infractions of military rules. Such training is no doubt particularly important where an offense charged against a soldier is purely military, such as disobedience of an order, leaving post, etc. But whether right or wrong, the premise underlying the constitutional method for determining guilt or innocence in federal courts is that laymen are better than specialists to perform this task. This idea is inherent in the institution of trial by jury.

Juries fairly chosen from different walks of life bring into the jury box a variety of different experiences, feelings, intuitions and habits. Such juries may reach completely different conclusions than would be reached by specialists in any single field, including specialists in the military field. On many occasions, fully known to the

Founders of this country, jurors - plain people - have manfully stood up in defense of liberty against the importunities of judges and despite prevailing hysteria and prejudices. . . . Unfortunately, instances could also be cited where jurors have themselves betrayed the cause of justice by verdicts based on prejudice or pressures. In such circumstances independent trial judges and independent appellate judges have a most important place under our constitutional plan since they have power to set aside convictions.

The 1950 Act here considered deprives of jury trial and sweeps under military jurisdiction over 3,000,000 persons who have become veterans since the Act became effective. That number is bound to grow from year to year; there are now more than 3,000,000 men and women in uniform. These figures point up what would be the enormous scope of a holding that Congress could subject every ex-serviceman and woman in the land to trial by court-martial for any alleged offense committed while he or she had been a member of the armed forces. Every veteran discharged since passage of the 1950 Act is subject to military trial for any offense punishable by as much as five years' imprisonment unless the offense is now punishable in a civilian court. And one need only glance at the Military Code to see what a vast number and variety of offenses are thus brought under military jurisdiction. Included within these are crimes such as murder, conspiracy, absence without leave, contempt toward officials, disrespect toward superior officers, willful or neglectful loss, damage, or destruction of government property, making false official statements, dueling, breach of the peace, forgery, fraud, assault, and many others. It is true that with reference to some of these offenses, very minor ones, veterans cannot now be tried because of a presidential order fixing the punishment for such offenses at less than five years. But that amelioration of the Military Code may be temporary, since punishment can be raised or lowered at the will of the President. It is also true that under the present law courts-martial have jurisdiction only if no civilian court does. But that might also be changed by Congress. Thus there is no justification for treating the Act as a mere minor increase of congressional power to expand military jurisdiction. It is a great change, both actually and potentially.

Fear has been expressed that if this law is not sustained discharged soldiers may escape punishment altogether for crimes they commit while in the service. But that fear is not warranted and was not shared by the Judge Advocate General of the Army who made a strong statement against passage of the law. He asked Congress to "confer jurisdiction upon Federal courts to try any person for an offense denounced by the [military] code if he is no longer subject thereto. This would be consistent with the fifth amendment of the Constitution." The Judge Advocate General went on to tell Congress that "If you expressly confer jurisdiction on the Federal courts to try such cases, you preserve the constitutional separation of military and civil courts, you save the military from a lot of unmerited grief, and you provide for a clean, constitutional method for disposing of such cases." It is conceded that it was wholly within the constitutional power of Congress to follow this suggestion and provide for federal district court trials of discharged soldiers accused of offenses committed while in the armed services. This concession is justified. There can be no valid argument, therefore, that civilian ex-servicemen must be tried by court-martial or not tried at all. If that is so it is only because Congress has not seen fit to subject them to trial in federal district courts.

None of the other reasons suggested by the Government are sufficient to justify a broad construction of the constitutional grant of power to Congress to regulate the armed forces. That provision itself does not empower Congress to deprive people of trials under Bill of Rights safeguards, and we are not willing to hold that power to circumvent those safeguards should be inferred through the Necessary and Proper Clause. It is impossible to think that the discipline of the Army is going to be disrupted, its morale impaired, or its orderly processes disturbed, by giving ex-servicemen the benefit of a civilian court trial when they are actually civilians. And we are not impressed by the fact that some other countries which do not have our Bill of Rights indulge in the practice of subjecting civilians who were once soldiers to trials by courts-martial instead of trials by civilian courts.

There are dangers lurking in military trials which were sought to be avoided by the Bill of Rights and Article 3 of our Constitution. Free countries of the world have tried to restrict military tribunals to the narrowest jurisdiction deemed absolutely essential to maintaining discipline among troops in active service. Even as late as the Seventeenth Century standing armies and courts-martial were not established institutions in England. Court-martial jurisdiction sprang from the belief that within the military ranks there is need for a prompt, ready-at-hand means of compelling obedience and order. But Army discipline will not be improved by court-martialing rather than trying by jury some civilian ex-soldier who has been wholly separated from the service for months, years or perhaps decades. Consequently considerations of discipline provide no excuse for new expansion of court-martial jurisdiction at the expense of the normal and constitutionally preferable system of trial by jury.

Determining the scope of the constitutional power of Congress to authorize trial by court-martial presents another instance calling for limitation to *"the least possible power adequate to the end proposed."* We hold that Congress cannot subject civilians like Toth to trial by court-martial. They, like other civilians, are entitled to have the benefit of safeguards afforded those tried in the regular courts authorized by Article 3 of the Constitution.

Reversed.

MARIJUANA

Timothy Leary v. U.S.

Whoever knowingly imports or smuggles into the United States marijuana ... shall be imprisoned.

The Marijuana Act

Dr. Timothy Leary attempted to cross from the United States to Mexico at the Laredo, Texas border in December 1965. Dr. Leary was denied entry into Mexico. United States customs inspectors asked Leary if he had anything to declare from his visit to Mexico. Leary explained that he had not been permitted into Mexico. A search of Leary's car revealed a small amount of marijuana. Dr. Leary was arrested for smuggling marijuana into the United States. Leary, the Harvard professor who had co-ined the sixty's drug phrase "Tune in, turn on, drop out" was tried on two marijuana-related charges in a Federal District Court. To the first charge of illegally smuggling marijuana into the United States, a violation of the Marijuana Act, Leary claimed in his defense that since Mexican customs had denied him entrance into Mexico, the marijuana found in his car could not have been smuggled. To the second charge of failing to pay the required marijuana tax, another violation of the Marijuana Tax Act, Leary argued that the Act itself was a violation of his Fifth Amendment privilege against self-incrimination. In order to be in full compliance with the Marijuana Tax Act, Leary argued, he would have had to incriminate himself. Dr. Timothy Leary was convicted of both charges and sentenced to the maximum penalty allowed by the law. Dr. Leary brought an appeal to the U.S. Court of Appeals, which upheld his marijuana convictions on both counts. Dr. Leary appealed for a reversal of his conviction to the United States Supreme Court.

Justice John Marshall Harlan delivered the 9-0 opinion of the Court on May 19, 1969. The edited text follows.

THE LEARY COURT

Chief Justice Earl Warren
Appointed Chief Justice by President Eisenhower
Served 1953 - 1969

Associate Justice Hugo Black
Appointed by President Franklin D. Roosevelt
Served 1937 - 1971

Associate Justice William O. Douglas
Appointed by President Franklin D. Roosevelt
Served 1939 - 1975

Associate Justice John Marshall Harlan
Appointed by President Eisenhower
Served 1955 - 1971

Associate Justice William Brennan
Appointed by President Eisenhower
Served 1956 - 1990

Associate Justice Potter Stewart
Appointed by President Eisenhower
Served 1958 - 1981

Associate Justice Byron White
Appointed by President Kennedy
Served 1962 - 1993

Associate Justice Abe Fortas
Appointed by President Lyndon Johnson
Served 1965 - 1969

Associate Justice Thurgood Marshall
Appointed by President Lyndon Johnson
Served 1967 - 1991

The unedited text of *Leary v. United States* can be found
on page 6, volume 395 of *United States Reports.*

LEARY v. UNITED STATES
MAY 19, 1969

JUSTICE HARLAN: This case presents constitutional questions arising out of the conviction of the petitioner, Dr. Timothy Leary, for violation of two federal statutes governing traffic in marihuana.

The circumstances surrounding [Leary's] conviction were as follows. On December 20, 1965 [Leary] left New York by automobile, intending a vacation trip to Yucatan, Mexico. He was accompanied by his daughter and son, both teenagers, and two other persons. On December 22, 1965, the party drove across the International Bridge between the United States and Mexico at Laredo, Texas. They stopped at the Mexican customs station and, after apparently being denied entry, drove back across the bridge. They halted at the American secondary inspection area, explained the situation to a customs inspector, and stated that they had nothing from Mexico to declare. The inspector asked them to alight, examined the interior of the car, and saw what appeared to be marihuana seeds on the floor. The inspector then received permission to search the car and passengers. Small amounts of marihuana were found on the car floor and in the glove compartment. A personal search of [Leary]'s daughter revealed a silver snuff box containing semi-refined marihuana and three partially smoked marihuana cigarettes.

[Leary] was indicted [charged] and tried before a jury in the Federal District Court for the Southern District of Texas, on three counts. First, it was alleged [charged] that he had knowingly smuggled marihuana into the United States. . . . Second, it was charged that he had knowingly transported and facilitated the transportation and concealment of marihuana which had been illegally imported or brought into the United States, with knowledge that it had been illegally imported or brought in.... Third, it was alleged that [Leary] was a transferee of marihuana and had knowingly transported, concealed, and facilitated the transportation and concealment of marihuana, without having paid the transfer tax imposed by the Marihuana Tax Act.

... [T]he District Court dismissed the first or smuggling counts. The jury found [him] guilty on the other two counts. He was tentatively sentenced to the maximum punishment, pending completion of a study and recommendations to be used by the District Court in fixing his final sentence. On appeal, the Court of Appeals for the Fifth Circuit affirmed [upheld]. That court subsequently denied a petition for rehearing....

We granted certiorari [agreed to hear the case] to consider two questions: (1) whether [Leary]'s conviction for failing to comply with the transfer tax provisions of the Marihuana Tax Act violated his Fifth Amendment privilege against self-incrimination; (2) whether [he] was denied due process by the application on the part of [the law] which provides that a defendant's possession of marihuana shall be deemed sufficient evidence that the marihuana was illegally imported or brought into the United States, and that the defendant knew of the illegal importation or bringing in, unless the defendant explains his possession to the satisfaction of the jury. For reasons which follow, we hold in favor of [Leary] on both issues and reverse the judgment of the Court of Appeals.

We consider first [Leary]'s claim that his conviction under the Marihuana Tax Act violated his privilege against self-incrimination.

[Leary] argues that reversal of his Marihuana Tax Act conviction is required by our decisions of last Term in *Marchetti v. United States, Grosso v. United States* and *Haynes v. United States.* In *Marchetti,* we held that a plea of the Fifth Amendment privilege provided a complete defense to a prosecution for failure to register and pay the occupational tax on wagers. We noted that wagering was a crime in almost every State, and that [the law] required that lists of wagering taxpayers be furnished to state and local prosecutors on demand. We concluded that compliance with the statute would have subjected [Marchetti] to a "real and appreciable" risk of self-incrimination. We further recognized that the occupational tax was not imposed in "'an essentially non-criminal and regulatory area . . . ,'" but was "directed to a 'selective group inherently suspect of criminal activities.'" We found that it would be inappropriate to impose restrictions on use of the information collected under the statute - a course urged by the Government as a means of removing the impact of the statute upon the privilege against self-incrimination - because of the evident congressional purpose to provide aid to prosecutors. We noted that, unlike the petitioner in *Shapiro v. United States, Marchetti* was not required to supply information which had a "public aspect" or was contained in records of the kind he customarily kept.

In *Grosso,* we held that the same considerations required that a claim of the privilege be a defense to prosecution under [the law], which imposes an excise tax on proceeds from wagering. And in *Haynes* we held for the same reasons that assertion of the Fifth Amendment privilege provided a defense to prosecution for possession of an unregistered weapon under the National Firearms Act, despite the fact that in "uncommon" instances registration under the statute would not be incriminating.

.... [It is] ... unlawful for a transferee required to pay the [Marijuana Tax Act's] Section 4741 (a) transfer tax either to acquire marihuana without having paid the tax or to transport, conceal, or facilitate the transportation or concealment of, any marihuana so acquired. [Leary] was convicted under Section 4744 (a). He conceded at trial that he had not obtained an order form or paid the transfer tax.

If read according to its terms, the Marihuana Tax Act compelled [Leary] to expose himself to a "real and appreciable" risk of self-incrimination, within the meaning of our decisions in *Marchetti, Grosso* and *Haynes*. Sections 4741-4742 required him, in the course of obtaining an order form, to identify himself not only as a transferee of marihuana but as a transferee who had not registered and paid the occupational tax under [Sections] 4751-4753. Section 4773 directed that this information be conveyed by the Internal Revenue Service to state and local law enforcement officials on request.

[Leary] had ample reason to fear that transmittal to such officials of the fact that he was a recent, unregistered transferee of marihuana "would surely prove a significant 'link in a chain' of evidence tending to establish his guilt" under the state marihuana laws then in effect. When [he] failed to comply with the Act, in late 1965, possession of any quantity of marihuana was apparently a crime in every one of the 50 States, including New York, where

[Leary] claimed the transfer occurred, and Texas, where he was arrested and convicted. It is true that almost all States, including New York and Texas, had exceptions making lawful, under specified conditions, possession of marihuana by: (1) state-licensed manufacturers and wholesalers; (2) apothecaries; (3) researchers; (4) physicians, dentists, veterinarians, and certain other medical personnel; (5) agents or employees of the foregoing persons or common carriers; (6) persons for whom the drug had been prescribed or to whom it had been given by an authorized medical person; and (7) certain public officials. However, individuals in the first four of these classes are among those compelled to register and pay the occupational tax . . . ; in consequence of having registered, they are required to pay only a $1 per ounce transfer tax . . . . It is extremely unlikely that such persons will remain unregistered, for failure to register renders them liable not only to an additional $99 per ounce transfer tax but also to severe criminal penalties. Persons in the last three classes mentioned above appear to be wholly exempt from the order form and transfer tax requirements.

Thus, at the time [Leary] failed to comply with the Act those persons who might legally possess marihuana under state law were virtually certain either to be registered . . . or to be exempt from the order form requirement. It follows that the class of possessors who were both unregistered and obliged to obtain an order form constituted a "selective group inherently suspect of criminal activities." Since compliance with the transfer tax provisions would have required [Leary] unmistakably to identify himself as a member of his "selective" and "suspect" group, we can only decide that when read according to their terms these provisions created a "real and appreciable" hazard of incrimination.

The Government, however, vigorously contends that when the Act is considered together with the accompanying regulations, and in light of existing administrative practice, its incriminatory aspect will be seen to vanish or shrink to less than constitutional proportions. The Government points first to regulations ... which provide that every applicant for registration ... must show that he is legally qualified to deal in marihuana according to the laws of the jurisdiction in which he is operating, and that the district director shall not permit an applicant to register until the director is satisfied that this is true. ...

The Government asserts that these regulations clearly signify that no person will be permitted to register unless his activities are permissible under the law of his jurisdiction, and that no one will be permitted to obtain an order form and prepay the transfer tax unless he has registered. The result, the Government contends, is simply to prohibit nonregistrants like [Leary] from dealing in marihuana at all. The Government further asserts that the administrative practice of the Internal Revenue Service and the Bureau of Narcotics has always been consistent with this interpretation, though it concedes that there apparently has never been an attempt by a nonregistrant to prepay the tax. The Government does admit uncertainty as to whether the fact of such an attempt would have been communicated to law enforcement officials; however, it points out that nothing in the statute or regulations appears to compel such disclosure. The Government argues that the regulations and administrative practice effectively refute the existence of a substantial hazard of incrimination at the time petitioner acquired marihuana: first, because a nonregistrant would have known that he could not obtain an order form and consequently never would have applied; second, because there was no substantial risk that an unsuccessful application would have been brought to the attention of law enforcement officials.

We cannot accept the Government's argument, for we find that Congress did intend that a nonregistrant should be able to obtain an order form and prepay the transfer tax. This congressional intent appears both from the language of the Act and from its legislative history.

We begin with the words of the statute. Section 4741(a), when read in conjunction with Section 4742, imposes a tax upon every transfer of marihuana, with a few exceptions not here relevant. Section 4741(a)(1) states that the tax on registrants shall be $1 per ounce and Section 4741(a)(2) that the tax on transfers to nonregistrants shall be $100 per ounce. Section 4741(b) states that "*[s]uch tax shall be paid by the transferee at the time of securing each order form* and shall be in addition to the price of such form." Since Section 4741(b) makes no distinction between the . . . tax on transfers to registrants and the . . . tax on transfers to nonregistrants, it seems clear that Congress contemplated that nonregistrant as well as registrant transferees should be able to obtain order forms and prepay the tax.

The legislative history also strongly indicates that the Act was intended merely to impose a very high tax on transfers to nonregistrants and not to prohibit such transfers entirely. As a taxing measure, the bill of course originated in the House of Representatives. At the start of the first hearing on the bill, before the House Ways and Means Committee, the committee chairman announced that he had introduced the bill at the request of the Secretary of the Treasury. The transfer provisions of the bill then read essentially as they do now. The first witness to appear before the Committee was the Treasury Department's Assistant General Counsel, Clinton M. Hester. He began by stating that the bill's purpose was "not only to raise revenue from the marihuana traffic, but also to discourage the current and widespread undesirable use of marihuana by smokers and drug addicts. . . ." He stated that in form the bill was a "synthesis" of the Harrison Narcotics Act, and the National Firearms Act. Both of these statutes compelled dealers in the respective goods to register and pay a special tax. Both prohibited transfer except in pursuance of a written form and imposed a transfer tax. However, the transfer provisions differed in that the Narcotics Act provided that no one except a registrant could legally obtain an order form, while the Firearms Act merely imposed a $200 tax upon each transfer of a firearm covered by the Act.

The Treasury witness explained that the marihuana tax bill generally followed the plan of the Narcotics Act insofar as it required dealers in marihuana to register and prohibited transfers except by order form. But he testified that because of constitutional doubts: "[a]t this point, this bill, like the National Firearms Act, departs from the plan of the Harrison Narcotics Act which limits the right to purchase narcotic drugs to those persons who are permitted to register under that act. . . .

"[I]n order to obviate the possibility of [an] attack upon the constitutionality of this bill, it, like the National Firearms Act, permits the transfer of marihuana to nonregistered persons upon the payment of a heavy transfer tax. The bill would permit the transfer of marihuana to anyone, but would impose a $100 per ounce tax upon a transfer to a person who might use it for purposes which are dangerous and harmful to the public. . . ."

Mr. Hester was also the first witness before a subcommittee of the Senate Finance Committee. There he testified in less detail, stating at different points that the purpose of the transfer provisions was "to discourage the widespread use of the drug by smokers and drug addicts," "to render extremely difficult the acquisition of marihuana by persons who desire it for illicit uses," "to prevent transfers to persons who would use marihuana for undesirable purposes," and "through the $100 transfer tax to prevent the drug from coming into the hands of those who will put it to illicit uses."

The House and Senate reports describe the purposes of the transfer provisions largely in the language of Mr. Hester's testimony. The House report declares that the purpose was "to discourage the widespread use of the drug by smokers and drug addicts," to "render extremely difficult the acquisition of marihuana by persons who desire it for illicit uses," and "through the $100 transfer tax to prevent the drug from coming into the hands of those who will put it to illicit uses." In discussing the issue of constitutionality, the report recites that "[t]he law is . . . settled that Congress has the power to enact a tax which is so heavy as to discourage the transactions or activities taxed" and states that "[t]hese cases sustain the $100 tax imposed . . . upon transfers . . . to unregistered persons." The Senate report, without discussing constitutionality, otherwise states the purpose of the transfer provisions in the very same words as the House report. Thus, the committee reports confirm Mr. Hester's account of the bill's purposes. In short, the legislative history fully accords with the statutory language.

Upon this evidence, we have no hesitation in concluding that the interpretation which the Government would give to the transfer provisions is, contrary to the manifest congressional intent that transfers to nonregistrants be taxed, not forbidden. Insofar as the regulations which require comparison of signatures necessarily compel the result urged by the Government, they must be regarded as contrary to the statute and hence beyond the scope of the regulation-making authority which was delegated by Congress. It is true that these regulations were promulgated in 1937, and that Congress re-enacted the entire Act in 1954, while they were in effect. However, the scanty legislative history accompanying that re-enactment gives no hint that Congress knew of these particular regulations, much less of the indirect impact which the Government now ascribes to them. . . .

[A]t the time [Leary] acquired marihuana he was confronted with a statute which on its face permitted him to acquire the drug legally, provided he paid the $100 per ounce transfer tax and gave incriminating information, and simultaneously with a system of regulations which, according to the Government, prohibited him from acquiring marihuana under any conditions. We have found those regulations so out of keeping with the statute as to be ultra vires [beyond its powers]. Faced with these conflicting commands, we think [Leary] would have been justified in giving precedence to the higher authority: the statute. "'[L]iteral and full compliance' with all the statutory requirements" would have entailed a very substantial risk of self-incrimination.

As has been noted, . . . Section 4773 requires that copies of order forms be kept available for inspection by state and local officials, and that copies be furnished to such officials on request. The House and Senate reports both state that one objective of the Act was "the development of an adequate means of publicizing dealings in marihuana in order to tax and control the traffic effectively." In short, we think the conclusion inescapable that the statute was aimed at bringing to light transgressions of the marihuana laws. . . .

Insofar as here relevant, Section 176a imposes criminal punishment upon every person who: "knowingly, with intent to defraud the United States, imports or brings into the United States marihuana contrary to law . . . , or receives, conceals, buys, sells, or in any manner facilitates the transportation, concealment, or sale of such marihuana after being imported or brought in, knowing the same to have been imported or brought into the United States contrary to law. . . ." A subsequent paragraph establishes the presumption now under scrutiny:

> "Whenever on trial for a violation of this subsection, the defendant is shown to have or to have had the marihuana in his possession, such possession shall be deemed sufficient evidence to authorize conviction unless the defendant explains his possession to the satisfaction of the jury."

The second count of the indictment charged [Leary] with having violated the "transportation" and "concealment" provisions of Section 176a. [He] admitted at trial that he had acquired marihuana in New York; had driven with it to Laredo, Texas; had continued across the bridge to the Mexican customs station; and then had returned to the United States. He further testified that he did not know where the marihuana he acquired had been grown.

In view of this testimony, the trial court instructed the jury that it might find [him] guilty of violating Section

176a on either of two alternative theories. Under the first or "South-North" theory, a conviction could have been based solely upon [Leary]'s own testimony that the marihuana had been brought back from Mexico into the United States and that with knowledge of that fact [he] had continued to transport it. Under the second or "North-South" theory, the conviction would have depended partly upon [Leary]'s testimony that he had transported the marihuana from New York to Texas and partly upon the challenged presumption.

.... By what criteria is the constitutionality of the Section 176a presumption to be judged?

Early decisions of this Court set forth a number of different standards by which to measure the validity of statutory presumptions.

.... [T]wo subsequent cases in which this Court ruled upon the constitutionality of criminal statutory presumptions involved companion sections of the Internal Revenue Code dealing with illegal stills. The presumption in *U.S. v. Gainey* was worded similarly to the one at issue here; it permitted a jury to infer from a defendant's presence at an illegal still that he was "carrying on" the business of a distiller "unless the defendant explains such presence to the satisfaction of the jury...."

We held that the *Gainey* presumption should be tested by the "rational connection" standard announced in *Tot.*

.... The presumption under attack in *United States v. Romano* was identical to that in *Gainey* except that it authorized the jury to infer from the defendant's presence at an illegal still that he had possession, custody, or control of the still. We held this presumption invalid. While stating that the result in *Gainey* was entirely justified because "[p]resence at an operating still is sufficient evidence to prove the charge of 'carrying on' because anyone present at the site is very probably connected with the illegal enterprise," we concluded:

> "Presence is relevant and admissible evidence in a trial on a possession charge; but absent some showing of the defendant's function at the still, its connection with possession is too tenuous to permit a reasonable inference of guilt - 'the inference of the one from proof of the other is arbitrary. . . .'

The upshot of *Tot, Gainey,* and *Romano* is, we think, that a criminal statutory presumption must be regarded as "irrational" or "arbitrary," and hence unconstitutional, unless it can at least be said with substantial assurance that the presumed fact is more likely than not to flow from the proved fact on which it is made to depend. And in the judicial assessment the congressional determination favoring the particular presumption must, of course, weigh heavily.

How does the Section 176a presumption fare under these standards?

So far as here relevant, the presumption authorizes the jury to infer from a defendant's possession of marihuana two necessary elements of the crime: (1) that the marihuana was imported or brought into the United States illegally; and (2) that the defendant knew of the unlawful importation or bringing in. [Leary] argues that neither inference is valid, citing undisputed testimony at his trial to the effect that marihuana will grow anywhere in the United States, and that some actually is grown here. The Government contends, on the other hand, that both inferences are permissible. For reasons that follow, we hold unconstitutional that part of the presumption which relates to a defendant's knowledge of illegal importation. Consequently, we do not reach the question of the validity of the "illegal importation" inference.

With regard to the "knowledge" presumption, we believe that *Tot* and *Romano* require that we take the statute at face value and ask whether it permits conviction upon insufficient proof of "knowledge," rather than inquire whether Congress might have made possession itself a crime. In order thus to determine the constitutionality of the "knowledge" inference, one must have direct or circumstantial data regarding the beliefs of marihuana users generally about the source of the drug they consume. Such information plainly is "not within specialized judicial competence or completely commonplace." . . . [T]he presumption apparently was enacted to relieve the Government of the burden of having to adduce [give] such evidence at every trail, and none was introduced by the prosecution at [Leary]'s trial. Since the determination of the presumption's constitutionality is "highly empirical," it follows that we must canvass the available, pertinent data.

. . . . As has been noted, we do not decide whether the presumption of illegal importation is itself constitutional. However, in view of the paucity of direct evidence as to the beliefs of marihuana smokers generally about the source of their marihuana, we have found it desirable to survey data concerning the proportion of domestically consumed marihuana which is of foreign origin, since in

the absence of better information the proportion of marihuana actually imported surely is relevant in deciding
whether marihuana possessors "know" that their marihuana is imported.

. . . . Near the outset of the Senate committee hearings,
the then Commissioner of Narcotics, Harry J. Anslinger,
estimated that 90% of all marihuana seized by federal authorities had been smuggled from Mexico, and that although "there is considerable volunteer growth from old
plantings in the Middle West . . . , [t]here is very little of
the local land used because it just does not have the advantage of the long summer growing, and [domestic mari-
huana] is not as potent as the Mexican drug." A number
of officials responsible for enforcing the narcotics laws in
various localities estimated that a similar proportion of
the marihuana consumed in their areas was of Mexican
origin.

On the other hand, written material inserted in the record
of the Senate hearings included former testimony of an
experienced federal customs agent before another Senate
committee, to the effect that high-quality marihuana was
being grown near the Texas cities of Laredo and Browns-
ville. A written report of the Ohio Attorney General recited that marihuana "may grow unnoticed along roadsides
and vacant lots in many parts of the country," and a Philadelphia Police Academy bulletin stated that: "Plenty of
[marihuana] is found growing in this city."

Examination of periodicals and books published since the
enactment of the presumption leaves no doubt that in
more than a dozen intervening years there have been
great changes in the extent and nature of marihuana use
in this country. With respect to quantity, one readily

available statistic is indicative: the amount of marihuana
seized in this country by federal authorities has jumped
from about 3,400 pounds in 1956 to about 61,400 pounds
in 1967. With regard to nature of use, the 1955 hearing
records and other reports portray marihuana smoking as
at that time an activity almost exclusively of unemployed
or menially employed members of racial minorities. Current periodicals and books, on the other hand, indicate
that marihuana smoking has become common on many
college campuses and among persons who have voluntarily
"dropped out" of American society in protest against its
values, and that marihuana smokers include a sizeable
number of young professional persons.

Despite these undoubted changes, the materials which we
have examined point quite strongly to the conclusion that
most domestically consumed marihuana is still of foreign
origin. During the six years 1962-1967, some 79% of all
marihuana seized by federal authorities was seized in attempted smuggling at ports and borders. The Government
informs us that a considerable part of the internally
seized marihuana bore indications of foreign origin.
While it is possible that these facts reflect only the de-
ployment of federal narcotics forces, rather than the actual proportion of imported to domestic marihuana, almost
all of the authorities which we have consulted confirm
that the preponderance of domestically consumed marihuana is grown in Mexico.

[Leary] makes much of statistics showing the number of
acres of domestic marihuana destroyed annually by state
and federal authorities, pointing out that if harvested the
destroyed acreage could in each year have accounted for
all marihuana estimated to have been consumed in the
United States, and that no one knows how many acres es-

cape destruction. However, several factors weaken this argument from domestic growth. First, the number of acres annually destroyed declined by a factor of three between 1959 and 1967, while during the same period the consumption of marihuana, as measured by federal seizures, rose twenty-fold. Assuming constant diligence on the part of those charged with destruction, this would indicate that in 1967 a much smaller share of the market was domestically supplied than in 1959. Second, while the total number of acres annually destroyed has indeed been large enough to furnish all domestically consumed marihuana, the state-by-state breakdowns which are available for the years 1964-1967 reveal that in each of those years more than 95% of the destroyed acreage was in two midwestern states, Illinois and Minnesota. The large, recurrent marihuana acreages discovered in those States can plausibly be ascribed to the "volunteer growth from old plantings in the Middle West" about which Commissioner Anslinger testified, while illicit cultivators of marihuana would be likely to choose States with sparser populations and more favorable climates. Third and last, reports of the Bureau of Narcotics and testimony of its agents indicate that in its far-reaching investigations the Bureau has never encountered a system for distributing sizable quantities of domestically grown marihuana. In contrast, the Bureau has found evidence of many large-scale distribution systems with sources in Mexico.

The Government urges that once it is concluded that most domestically consumed marihuana comes from abroad - a conclusion which we think is warranted by the data just examined - we must uphold the "knowledge" part of the presumption in light of this Court's decision in *Yee Hem v. United States*. In that case, the Court sustained [upheld] a presumption which was virtually identical to

the one at issue here except that the forbidden substance
was smoking opium rather than marihuana. With respect
to the inference of knowledge from possession which was
authorized by that presumption, the Court said:

> "Legitimate possession [of opium], unless for me-
> dicinal use, is so highly improbable that to say to
> any person who obtains the outlawed commodity,
> 'since you are bound to know that it cannot be
> brought into this country at all, except under reg-
> ulation for medicinal use, you must at your peril
> ascertain and be prepared to show the facts and
> circumstances which rebut, or tend to rebut, the
> natural inference of unlawful importation, or
> your knowledge of it,' is not such an unreasona-
> ble requirement as to cause it to fall outside the
> constitutional power of Congress."

The Government contends that *Yee Hem* requires us to
read the Section 176a presumption as intended to put every marihuana smoker on notice that he must be prepared
to show that any marihuana in his possession was not illegally imported, and that since the possessor is the person
most likely to know the marihuana's origin it is not unfair
to require him to adduce evidence on that point. However, we consider that this approach, which closely resembles
the test of comparative convenience in the production of
evidence, was implicitly abandoned in *Tot v. United
States*. . . . [T]he Tot Court confronted a presumption
which allowed a jury to infer from possession of a fire-
arm that it was received in interstate commerce. Despite
evidence that most States prohibited unregistered and un-
recorded acquisition of firearms, the Court did not read
the statute as notifying possessors that they must be prepared to show that they received their weapons in intra-

state transactions, as *Yee Hem* would seem to dictate. Instead, while recognizing that "the defendants . . . knew better than anyone else whether they acquired the firearms or ammunition in interstate commerce," the Court held that because of the danger of overreaching it was incumbent upon the prosecution to demonstrate that the inference was permissible before the burden of coming forward could be placed upon the defendant. This was a matter which the *Yee Hem* Court either thought it unnecessary to consider or assumed when it described the inference as "natural."

We therefore must consider in detail whether the available evidence supports the conclusion that the "knowledge" part of the Section 176a presumption is constitutional under the standard established in *Tot* and adhered to in *Gainey* and *Romano* - that is, whether it can be said with substantial assurance that one in possession of marihuana is more likely than not to know that his marihuana was illegally imported.

Even if we assume that the previously assembled data are sufficient to justify the inference of illegal importation, it by no means follows that a majority of marihuana possessors "know" that their marihuana was illegally imported. Any such proposition would depend upon an intermediate premise: that most marihuana possessors are aware of the level of importation and have deduced that their own marihuana was grown abroad. This intermediate step might be thought justified by common sense if it were proved that little or no marihuana is grown in this country. Short of such a showing, not here present, we do not believe that the inference of knowledge can be sustained solely because of the assumed validity of the "importation" presumption.

Once it is established that a significant percentage of domestically consumed marihuana may not have been imported at all, then it can no longer be postulated, without proof, that possessors will be even roughly aware of the proportion actually imported. We conclude that in order to sustain the inference of knowledge we must find on the basis of the available materials that a majority of marihuana possessors either are cognizant of the apparently high rate of importation or otherwise have become aware that *their* marihuana was grown abroad.

We can imagine five ways in which a possessor might acquire such knowledge: (1) he might be aware of the proportion of domestically consumed marihuana which is smuggled from abroad and deduce that his was illegally imported; (2) he might have smuggled the marihuana himself; (3) he might have learned by indirect means that the marihuana consumed in his locality or furnished by his supplier was smuggled from abroad; (4) he might have specified foreign marihuana when making his "buy," or might have been told the source of the marihuana by his supplier; (5) he might be able to tell the source from the appearance, packaging, or taste of the marihuana itself.

.... We conclude that the "knowledge" aspect of the Section 176a presumption cannot be upheld without making serious incursions into the teachings of *Tot, Gainey,* and *Romano.* In the context of this part of the statute, those teachings require that it be determined with substantial assurance that at least a majority of marihuana possessors have learned of the foreign origin of their marihuana through one or more of [these five] ways....

We find it impossible to make such a determination. As we have seen, the materials at our disposal leave us at large to estimate even roughly the proportion of marihuana possessors who have learned in one way or another the origin of their marihuana. It must also be recognized that a not inconsiderable proportion of domestically consumed marihuana appears to have been grown in this country, and that its possessors must be taken to have "known," if anything, that their marihuana was *not* illegally imported. In short, it would be no more than speculation were we to say that even as much as a majority of possessors "knew" the source of their marihuana.

.... Congress, no less than we, is subject to constitutional requirements, and in this instance the legislative record falls even shorter of furnishing an adequate foundation for the "knowledge" presumption than do the more extensive materials we have examined.

We thus cannot escape the duty of setting aside [Leary]'s conviction under Count 2 of this indictment.

.... [W]e reverse outright the judgment of conviction on Count 3 of the indictment.... [W]e reverse the judgment of conviction on Count 2 and remand [return] the case to the Court of Appeals for further proceedings consistent with this opinion. We are constrained to add that nothing in what we hold today implies any constitutional disability in Congress to deal with the marihuana traffic by other means. ...

BIRTH CONTROL

Eisenstadt v. Baird

Whoever sells, lends, gives away, exhibits or offers to sell an instrument, article, drug or medicine for the prevention of contraception . . . [except physicians for the use of married persons] . . . *shall be punished by imprisonment in the state prison for not more than five years.* **The Massachusetts Birth Control Act**

William Baird, a birth control lecturer and advocate, was tried and convicted of violating certain provisions of the Massachusetts Birth Control Act. This Act, part of the Massachusetts "Crimes Against Chastity, Morality, Decency and Good Order" made it a felony, punishable by a maximum of five years in prison, for anyone other than a health care professional to exhibit or distribute birth control devices to anyone other than married persons.

In 1966 William Baird, a lay expert on birth control, addressed an audience at Boston University. During the lecture Baird displayed various contraceptives. At the close of his lecture Baird invited the audience to help themselves to these contraceptives. Baird personally "gave away" a contraceptive to one woman. He was arrested by Suffolk County Sheriff Thomas Eisenstadt. Baird was convicted in Massachusetts Superior Court of violating the Massachusetts Birth Control Act by "giving away" a birth control device to an unmarried person. On appeal the Massachusetts Supreme Court upheld the "giving away" conviction. Baird appealed for a reversal to a U.S. District Court, which denied his request. On appeal the U.S. Court of Appeals granted his release. Massachusetts appealed to the United States Supreme Court.

Justice William Brennan delivered the 6-1 (Justices Rehnquist and Powell not participating) opinion of the Court on March 22, 1972. The edited text follows.

THE BAIRD COURT

Chief Justice Warren Burger
Appointed Chief Justice by President Nixon
Served 1969 - 1986

Associate Justice William O. Douglas
Appointed by President Franklin D. Roosevelt
Served 1939 - 1975

Associate Justice William Brennan
Appointed by President Eisenhower
Served 1956 - 1990

Associate Justice Potter Stewart
Appointed by President Eisenhower
Served 1958 - 1981

Associate Justice Byron White
Appointed by President Kennedy
Served 1962 - 1993

Associate Justice Thurgood Marshall
Appointed by President Lyndon Johnson
Served 1967 - 1991

Associate Justice Harry Blackmun
Appointed by President Nixon
Served 1970 - 1994

The unedited text of *Eisenstadt v. Baird* can be found
on page 31, volume 438 of *United States Reports.*

EISENSTADT v. BAIRD
MARCH 22, 1972

JUSTICE BRENNAN: Appellee William Baird was convicted at a bench trial in the Massachusetts Superior
Court under Massachusetts General Laws, first, for exhibiting contraceptive articles in the course of delivering a
lecture on contraception to a group of students at Boston
University and, second, for giving a young woman a pack-
age of Emko vaginal foam at the close of his address. The
Massachusetts Supreme Judicial Court unanimously set
aside the conviction for exhibiting contraceptives on the
ground that it violated Baird's First Amendment rights,
but by a four-to-three vote sustained [upheld] the conviction for giving away the foam. Baird subsequently filed a
petition for a federal writ of habeas corpus [a request to
bring a case before a court], which the District Court dismissed. On appeal however, the Court of Appeals for the
First Circuit vacated [threw out] the dismissal and remanded [sent back] the action with directions to grant the
writ discharging Baird. This appeal by the Sheriff of Suffolk County, Massachusetts, followed, and we noted probable jurisdiction [authority]. We affirm [uphold].

Massachusetts General Laws under which Baird was convicted, provides a maximum five-year term of imprisonment for "whoever ... gives away ... any drug, medicine,
instrument or article whatever for the prevention of conception," except as authorized in Section 21A. Under Section 21A, "[a] registered physician may administer to or
prescribe for any married person drugs or articles intended for the prevention of pregnancy or conception. [And
a] registered pharmacist actually engaged in the business
of pharmacy may furnish such drugs or articles to any
married person presenting a prescription from a regis-

tered physician." As interpreted by the State Supreme Judicial Court, these provisions make it a felony for anyone, other than a registered physician or pharmacist acting in accordance with the terms of Section 21A, to dispense any article with the intention that it be used for the prevention of conception. The statutory scheme distinguishes among three distinct classes of distributees - *first*, married persons may obtain contraceptives to prevent pregnancy, but only from doctors or druggists on prescription; *second*, single persons may not obtain contraceptives from anyone to prevent pregnancy; and *third*, married or single persons may obtain contraceptives from anyone to prevent, not pregnancy, but the spread of disease. This construction of state law is, of course, binding on us.

The legislative purposes that the statute is meant to serve are not altogether clear. In *Commonwealth v. Baird*, the Supreme Judicial Court noted only the State's interest in protecting the health of its citizens: "[T]he prohibition in Section 21," the court declared, "is directly related to" the State's goal of "preventing the distribution of articles designed to prevent conception which may have undesirable, if not dangerous, physical consequences." In a subsequent decision, *Sturgis v. Attorney General*, the court, however, found "a second and more compelling ground for upholding the statute" - namely, to protect morals through "regulating the private sexual lives of single persons." The Court of Appeals, for reasons that will appear, did not consider the promotion of health or the protection of morals through the deterrence of fornication to be the legislative aim. Instead, the court concluded that the statutory goal was to limit contraception in and of itself - a purpose that the court held conflicted "with fundamental human rights" under *Griswold v. Connecticut*, where this Court struck down Connecticut's prohibition against the use of contraceptives as an unconstitutional infringement of the right of marital privacy.

We agree that the goals of deterring premarital sex and regulating the distribution of potentially harmful articles cannot reasonably be regarded as legislative aims of Sections 21 and 21A. And we hold that the statute, viewed as a prohibition on contraception per se, violates the rights of single persons under the Equal Protection Clause of the Fourteenth Amendment.

We address at the outset appellant's [Eisenstadt's] contention that Baird does not have standing [the legal right] to assert the rights of unmarried persons denied access to contraceptives because he was neither an authorized distributor under Section 21A nor a single person unable to obtain contraceptives. . . . [Eisenstadt] contends that Baird's conviction rests on the restriction in Section 21A on permissible distributors and that that restriction serves a valid health interest independent of the limitation on authorized distributees. [He] urges, therefore, that Baird's action in giving away the foam fell squarely within the conduct that the legislature meant and had power to prohibit and that Baird should not be allowed to attack the statute in its application to potential recipients. In any event, [Eisenstadt] concludes, since Baird was not himself a single person denied access to contraceptives, he should not be heard to assert their rights. We cannot agree.

The Court of Appeals held that the statute under which Baird was convicted is not a health measure. If that view is correct, we do not see how Baird may be prevented, because he was neither a doctor nor a druggist, from attacking the statute in its alleged discriminatory application to potential distributees. We think, too, that our self-imposed rule against the assertion of third-party rights must be relaxed in this case just as in *Griswold v. Connecticut.* ... [I]n *Barrows v. Jackson,* a seller of land was entitled to defend against an action for damages for breach of a racially restrictive covenant on the ground that enforcement of the covenant violated the equal protection rights of prospective non-Caucasian purchasers. The relationship there between the defendant and those whose rights he sought to assert was not simply the fortuitous connection between a vendor and potential vendees, but the relationship between one who acted to protect the rights of a minority and the minority itself. And so here the relationship between Baird and those whose rights he seeks to assert is not simply that between a distributor and potential distributees, but that between an advocate of the rights of persons to obtain contraceptives and those desirous of doing so. The very point of Baird's giving away the vaginal foam was to challenge the Massachusetts statute that limited access to contraceptives.

In any event, more important than the nature of the relationship between the litigant and those whose rights he seeks to assert is the impact of the litigation on the third-party interests. In *Griswold,* the Court stated: "The rights of husband and wife, pressed here, are likely to be diluted or adversely affected unless those rights are considered in a suit involving those who have this kind of confidential relation to them." A similar situation obtains here. Enforcement of the Massachusetts statute will materially impair the ability of single persons to obtain contraceptives. In fact, the case for according standing to assert third-party rights is stronger in this regard here than in *Griswold* because unmarried persons denied access to contraceptives in Massachusetts, unlike the users of contraceptives in Connecticut, are not themselves subject to prosecution and, to that extent, are denied a forum in which to assert their own rights. The Massachusetts statute, unlike the Connecticut law considered in *Griswold*, prohibits, not use, but distribution.

For the foregoing reasons we hold that Baird, who is now in a position, and plainly has an adequate incentive, to assert the rights of unmarried persons denied access to contraceptives, has standing to do so.....

The basic principles governing application of the Equal Protection Clause of the Fourteenth Amendment are familiar. As the Chief Justice only recently explained in *Reed v. Reed*:

> "In applying that clause, this Court has consistently recognized that the Fourteenth Amendment does not deny to States the power to treat different classes of persons in different ways. The Equal Protection Clause of that amendment does, however, deny to States the power to legislate that different treatment be accorded to persons placed by a statute into different classes on the basis of criteria wholly unrelated to the objective of that statute. A classification 'must be reasonable, not arbitrary, and must rest upon some ground of difference having a fair and substantial relation to the object of the legislation, so that all persons similarly circumstanced shall be treated alike.'"

The question for our determination in this case is whether there is some ground of difference that rationally explains the different treatment accorded married and unmarried persons under Massachusetts General Laws. For the reasons that follow, we conclude that no such ground exists.

First. Section 21 stems from Massachusetts Statute 1879, which prohibited, without exception, distribution of articles intended to be used as contraceptives. In *Commonwealth v. Allison,* the Massachusetts Supreme Judicial Court explained that the law's "plain purpose is to protect purity, to preserve chastity, to encourage continence and self restraint, to defend the sanctity of the home, and thus to engender in the State and nation a virile and virtuous race of men and women." Although the State clearly abandoned that purpose with the enactment of Section 21A, at least insofar as the illicit sexual activities of married persons are concerned, the court reiterated in *Sturgis v. Attorney General,* that the object of the legislation is to discourage premarital sexual intercourse. Conceding that the State could, consistently with the Equal Protection Clause, regard the problems of extramarital and premarital sexual relations as "[e]vils . . . of different dimensions and proportions, requiring different remedies," we cannot agree that the deterrence of premarital sex may reasonably be regarded as the purpose of the Massachusetts law.

It would be plainly unreasonable to assume that Massachusetts has prescribed pregnancy and the birth of an unwanted child as punishment for fornication, which is a misdemeanor under Massachusetts General Laws. Aside from the scheme of values that assumption would attribute to the State, it is abundantly clear that the effect of the ban on distribution of contraceptives to unmarried persons has at best a marginal relation to the proffered objective. What Justice Goldberg said in *Griswold v. Connecticut,* concerning the effect of Connecticut's prohibition on the use of contraceptives in discouraging extramarital sexual relations, is equally applicable here. "The rationality of this justification is dubious, particularly in light of the admitted widespread availability to all persons in the State of Connecticut, unmarried as well as married, of birth-control devices for the prevention of disease, as distinguished from the prevention of conception." Like Connecticut's laws, Sections 21 and 21A do not at all regulate the distribution of contraceptives when they are to be used to prevent, not pregnancy, but the spread of disease. Nor, in making contraceptives available to married persons without regard to their intended use, does Massachusetts attempt to deter married persons from engaging in illicit sexual relations with unmarried persons. Even on the assumption that the fear of pregnancy operates as a deterrent to fornication, the Massachusetts statute is thus so riddled with exceptions that deterrence of premarital sex cannot reasonably be regarded as its aim.

Moreover, Sections 21 and 21A on their face have a dubious relation to the State's criminal prohibition on fornication. As the Court of Appeals explained, "Fornication is a misdemeanor [in Massachusetts], entailing a thirty dollar fine, or three months in jail. Violation of the present statute is a felony, punishable by five years in prison. We find it hard to believe that the legislature adopted a statute carrying a five-year penalty for its possible, obviously by no means fully effective, deterrence of the commission of a ninety-day misdemeanor." Even conceding the legislature a full measure of discretion in fashioning means to prevent fornication, and recognizing that the State may seek to deter prohibited conduct by punishing more severely those who facilitate than those who actually engage in its commission, we, like the Court of Appeals, cannot believe that in this instance Massachusetts has chosen to expose the aider and abetter who simply *gives away* a contraceptive to *20* times the *90-day* sentence of the offender himself. The very terms of the State's criminal statutes, coupled with the de minimis [insignificant] effect of Sections 21 and 21A in deterring fornication, thus compel the conclusion that such deterrence cannot reasonably be taken as the purpose of the ban on distribution of contraceptives to unmarried persons.

Second. Section 21A was added to the Massachusetts General Laws by Statute 1966. The Supreme Judicial Court in *Commonwealth v. Baird,* held that the purpose of the amendment was to serve the health needs of the community by regulating the distribution of potentially harmful articles. It is plain that Massachusetts had no such purpose in mind before the enactment of Section 21A. As the Court of Appeals remarked, "Consistent with the fact that the statute was contained in a chapter dealing with 'Crimes Against Chastity, Morality, Decency and Good Order,' it was cast only in terms of morals. A physician was forbidden to prescribe contraceptives even when needed for the protection of health. Nor did the Court of Appeals "believe that the legislature [in enacting Section 21A] suddenly reversed its field and developed an interest in health. Rather, it merely made what it thought to be the precise accommodation necessary to escape the Griswold ruling."

Again, we must agree with the Court of Appeals. If health were the rationale of Section 21A, the statute would be both discriminatory and overbroad. Dissenting in *Commonwealth v. Baird,* Justices Whittemore and Cutter stated that they saw "in Section 21 and Section 21A, read together, no public health purpose. If there is need to have a physician prescribe (and a pharmacist dispense) contraceptives, that need is as great for unmarried persons as for married persons." The Court of Appeals added: "If the prohibition [on distribution to unmarried persons] . . . is to be taken to mean that the same physician who can prescribe for married patients does not have sufficient skill to protect the health of patients who lack a marriage certificate, or who may be currently divorced, it is illogical to the point of irrationality." Furthermore, we must join the Court of Appeals in noting that not all contraceptives are potentially dangerous. As a result, if the Massachusetts statute were a health measure, it would not only invidiously discriminate against the unmarried, but also be overbroad with respect to the married, a fact that the Supreme Judicial Court itself seems to have conceded in *Sturgis v. Attorney General*, where it noted that "it may well be that certain contraceptive medication and devices constitute no hazard to health, in which event it could be argued that the statute swept too broadly in its prohibition." "In this posture," as the Court of Appeals concluded, "it is impossible to think of the statute as intended as a health measure for the unmarried, and it is almost as difficult to think of it as so intended even as to the married."

But if further proof that the Massachusetts statute is not a health measure is necessary, the argument of Justice Spiegel, who also dissented in *Commonwealth v. Baird*, is conclusive: "It is at best a strained conception to say that the Legislature intended to prevent the distribution of articles 'which may have undesirable, if not dangerous, physical consequences.' If that was the Legislature's goal, Section 21 is not required" in view of the federal and state laws *already* regulating the distribution of harmful drugs. We conclude, accordingly, that, despite the statute's superficial earmarks as a health measure, health, on the face of the statute, may no more reasonably be regarded as its purpose than the deterrence of premarital sexual relations.

Third. If the Massachusetts statute cannot be upheld as a deterrent to fornication or as a health measure, may it, nevertheless, be sustained simply as a prohibition on contraception? The Court of Appeals analysis "led inevitably to the conclusion that, so far as morals are concerned, it is contraceptives per se that are considered immoral - to the extent that *Griswold* will permit such a declaration." The Court of Appeals went on to hold:

> "To say that contraceptives are immoral as such, and are to be forbidden to unmarried persons who will nevertheless persist in having intercourse, means that such persons must risk for themselves an unwanted pregnancy, for the child, illegitimacy, and for society, a possible obligation of support. Such a view of morality is not only the very mirror image of sensible legislation; we consider that it conflicts with fundamental human rights. In the absence of demonstrated harm, we hold it is beyond the competency of the state."

We need not and do not, however, decide that important question in this case because, whatever the rights of the individual to access to contraceptives may be, the rights must be the same for the unmarried and the married alike.

If under *Griswold* the distribution of contraceptives to married persons cannot be prohibited, a ban on distribution to unmarried persons would be equally impermissible. It is true that in *Griswold* the right of privacy in question inhered in the marital relationship. Yet the marital couple is not an independent entity with a mind and heart of its own, but an association of two individuals each with a separate intellectual and emotional makeup. If the right of privacy means anything, it is the right of

the *individual,* married or single, to be free from unwarranted governmental intrusion into matters so fundamentally affecting a person as the decision whether to bear or
beget a child.

On the other hand, if *Griswold* is no bar to a prohibition
on the distribution of contraceptives, the State could not,
consistently with the Equal Protection Clause, outlaw distribution to unmarried but not to married persons.   In
each case the evil, as perceived by the State, would be
identical, and the underinclusion would be invidious. Justice Jackson, concurring in *Railway Express Agency v.
New York,* made the point:

> "The framers of the Constitution knew, and we
> should not forget today, that there is no more ef-
> fective practical guaranty against arbitrary and
> unreasonable government than to require that the
> principles of law which officials would impose
> upon a minority must be imposed generally.
> Conversely, nothing opens the door to arbitrary
> action so effectively as to allow those officials to
> pick and choose only a few to whom they will ap-
> ply legislation and thus to escape the political ret-
> ribution that might be visited upon them if larger
> numbers were affected. Courts can take no bet-
> ter measure to assure that laws will be just than
> to require that laws be equal in operation."

Although Justice Jackson's comments had reference to administrative regulations, the principle he affirmed has
equal application to the legislation here. We hold that by
providing dissimilar treatment for married and unmarried
persons who are similarly situated, Sections 21 and 21A

violate the Equal Protection Clause. The judgment of the Court of Appeals is affirmed.

BASEBALL

Flood v. Kuhn

The Player agrees that this contract may be assigned by the Club (and reassigned by any other Club) to any other Club in accordance with the Major League Rules and the Professional Baseball Rules. - **The Reserve Clause**

Baseball's Reserve Clause, written into all professional baseball players' contracts since 1887, bound a baseball player to the professional team with which he had signed for the rest of his career. The Reserve Clause was clearly a violation of federal antitrust laws. In 1922 Justice Oliver Wendell Holmes ruled in the *Federal Baseball Club* decision that baseball was exempt from the antitrust laws.

Curtis Charles Flood was an exceptional center fielder for the St. Louis Cardinals who, for the twelve years between 1958 and 1969, batted .293 and won and seven Gold Gloves. In 1969 Flood, without his consent or knowledge, was traded to the Philadelphia Phillies. Curt Flood wrote to Bowie Kuhn, the Baseball Commissioner: "[I am not] a piece of property to be bought and sold." He asked to be made a free agent which would have voided the Reserve Clause. Kuhn told Flood to play for Philadelphia or not at all. Arguing the Reserve Clause in his contract was a violation of federal antitrust laws and that the almost fifty-year-old *Federal Baseball* antitrust exemption should be reversed, Flood sued the Commissioner, the National and American Leagues, and all 24 major league baseball clubs. After a trial in U.S. District Court, the Reserve Clause and baseball's antitrust exemption were upheld. Flood took an appeal to the U.S. Court of Appeals, which affirmed. Flood appealed to the U.S. Supreme Court.

Justice Harry Blackmun delivered the 5-3 opinion (Justice Powell did not participate) of the Court on June 19, 1972. The edited text follows.

THE FLOOD COURT

Chief Justice Warren Burger
Appointed Chief Justice by President Nixon
Served 1969 - 1986

Associate Justice William O. Douglas
Appointed by President Franklin D. Roosevelt
Served 1939 - 1975

Associate Justice William Brennan
Appointed by President Eisenhower
Served 1956 - 1990

Associate Justice Potter Stewart
Appointed by President Eisenhower
Served 1958 - 1981

Associate Justice Byron White
Appointed by President Kennedy
Served 1962 - 1993

Associate Justice Thurgood Marshall
Appointed by President Lyndon Johnson
Served 1967 - 1991

Associate Justice Harry Blackmun
Appointed by President Nixon
Served 1970 - 1994

Associate Justice William Rehnquist
Appointed Associate Justice by President Nixon
Served 1971 -

The unedited text of *Flood v. Kuhn* can be found
on page 258, volume 407 of *United States Reports.*

FLOOD v. KUHN
JUNE 19, 1972

JUSTICE BLACKMUN: For the third time in 50 years the Court is asked specifically to rule that professional baseball's reserve system is within the reach of the federal antitrust laws....

It is a century and a quarter since the New York Nine defeated the Knickerbockers 23 to 1 on Hoboken's Elysian Fields June 19, 1846, with Alexander Jay Cartwright as the instigator and the umpire. The teams were amateur, but the contest marked a significant date in baseball's beginnings. That early game led ultimately to the development of professional baseball and its tightly organized structure.

The Cincinnati Red Stockings came into existence in 1869 upon an outpouring of local pride. With only one Cincinnatian on the payroll, this professional team traveled over 11,000 miles that summer, winning 56 games and tying one. Shortly thereafter, on St. Patrick's Day in 1871, the National Association of Professional Baseball Players was founded and the professional league was born.

The ensuing colorful days are well known. The ardent follower and the student of baseball know of General Abner Doubleday; the formation of the National League in 1876; Chicago's supremacy in the first year's competition under the leadership of Al Spalding and with Cap Anson at third base; the formation of the American Association and then of the Union Association in the 1880's; the introduction of Sunday baseball; interleague warfare with cut-rate admission prices and player raiding; the development of the reserve "clause"; the emergence in 1885 of the Brotherhood of Professional Ball Players, and in 1890 of the Players League; the appearance of the American League, or "junior circuit," in 1901, rising from the minor Western Association; the first World Series in 1903, disruption in 1904, and the Series' resumption in 1905; the short-lived Federal League on the majors' scene during World War I years; the troublesome and discouraging episode of the 1919 Series; the home run ball; the shifting of franchises; the expansion of the leagues; the installation in 1965 of the major league draft of potential new players; and the formation of the Major League Baseball Players Association in 1966.

Then there are the many names, celebrated for one reason or another, that have sparked the diamond and its environs and that have provided tinder for recaptured thrills, for reminiscence and comparisons, and for conversation and anticipation in-season and off-season: Ty Cobb, Babe Ruth, Tris Speaker, Walter Johnson, Henry Chadwick, Eddie Collins, Lou Gehrig, Grover Cleveland Alexander, Rogers Hornsby, Harry Hooper, Goose Goslin, Jackie Robinson, Honus Wagner, Joe McCarthy, John McGraw, Deacon Phillippe, Rube Marquard, Christy Mathewson, Tommy Leach, Big Ed Delahanty, Davy Jones, Germany Schaefer, King Kelly, Big Dan Brouthers, Wahoo Sam Crawford, Wee Willie Keeler, Big Ed Walsh, Jimmy Austin, Fred Snodgrass, Satchel Paige, Hugh Jennings, Fred Merkle, Iron Man McGinnity, Three-Finger Brown, Harry and Stan Coveleski, Connie Mack, Al Bridwell, Red Ruffing, Amos Rusie, Cy Young, Smokey Joe Wood, Chief Meyers, Chief Bender, Bill Klem, Hans Lobert, Johnny Evers, Joe Tinker, Roy Campanella, Miller Huggins, Rube Bressler, Dizzy Vance, Edd Roush, Bill Wambsganss, Clark Griffith, Branch Rickey, Frank Chance, Cap Anson, Nap Lajoie, Sad Sam Jones, Bob O'Farrell, Lefty O'Doul, Bobby Veach, Willie Kamm, Heinie Groh, Lloyd and Paul Waner, Stuffy McInnis, Charles Comiskey, Roger Bresnahan, Bill Dickey, Zack Wheat, George Sisler, Charlie Gehringer, Eppa Rixey, Harry Heilmann, Fred Clarke, Dizzy Dean, Hank Greenberg, Pie Traynor, Rube Waddell, Bill Terry, Carl Hubbell, Old Hoss Radbourne, Moe Berg, Rabbit Maranville, Jimmie Foxx, Lefty Grove. The list seems endless.

And one recalls the appropriate reference to the "World Serious," attributed to Ring Lardner, Sr.; Ernest L. Thayer's "Casey at the Bat"; the ring of "Tinker to Evers to Chance"; and all the other happenings, habits, and superstitions about and around baseball that made it the "national pastime" or, depending upon the point of view, "the great American tragedy."

The petitioner, Curtis Charles Flood, born in 1938, began his major league career in 1956 when he signed a contract with the Cincinnati Reds for a salary of $4,000 for the season. He had no attorney or agent to advise him on that occasion. He was traded to the St. Louis Cardinals before the 1958 season. Flood rose to fame as a center fielder with the Cardinals during the years 1958-1969. In those 12 seasons he compiled a batting average of .293. His best offensive season was 1967 when he achieved .335. He was .301 or better in six of the 12 St. Louis years. He participated in the 1964, 1967, and 1968 World Series. He played errorless ball in the field in 1966, and once enjoyed 223 consecutive errorless games. Flood has received seven Golden Glove Awards. He was co-captain of his team from 1965-1969. He ranks among the 10 major league outfielders possessing the highest lifetime fielding averages.

Flood's St. Louis compensation for the years shown was: 1961 - $13,500 (including a bonus for signing); 1962 - $16,000; 1963 - $17,500; 1964 - $23,000; 1965 - $35,000; 1966 - $45,000; 1967 - $50,000; 1968 - $72,500; 1969 - $90,000. These figures do not include any so-called fringe benefits or World Series shares.

But at the age of 31, in October 1969, Flood was traded to the Philadelphia Phillies of the National League in a multi-player transaction. He was not consulted about the trade. He was informed by telephone and received formal notice only after the deal had been consummated. In December he complained to the Commissioner of Baseball and asked that he be made a free agent and be placed at liberty to strike his own bargain with any other major league team. His request was denied.

Flood then instituted this antitrust suit in January 1970 in federal court for the Southern District of New York. The defendants . . . were the Commissioner of Baseball, the presidents of the two major leagues, and the 24 major league clubs. In general, the complaint charged violations of the federal antitrust laws and civil rights statutes, violation of state statutes and the common law, and the imposition of a form of peonage and involuntary servitude contrary to the Thirteenth Amendment. . . .

Flood declined to play for Philadelphia in 1970, despite a $100,000 salary offer, and he sat out the year. After the season was concluded, Philadelphia sold its rights to Flood to the Washington Senators. Washington [agreed to] a salary of $110,000 [for 1971]. Flood started the season but, apparently because he was dissatisifed with his performance, he left the Washington club on April 27, early in the campaign. He has not played baseball since then.

Judge Cooper, in a detailed opinion, first denied a prelimi-
nary injunction [court order stopping an action], observing on the way:

> "Baseball has been the national pastime for over
> one hundred years and enjoys a unique place in
> our American heritage. Major league profession-
> al baseball is avidly followed by millions of fans,
> looked upon with fervor and pride and provides a
> special source of inspiration and competitive
> team spirit especially for the young.

> "Baseball's status in the life of the nation is so
> pervasive that it would not strain credulity to say
> the Court can take judicial notice that baseball is
> everybody's business. To put it mildly and with
> restraint, it would be unfortunate indeed if a fine
> sport and profession, which brings surcease from
> daily travail and an escape from the ordinary to
> most inhabitants of this land, were to suffer in
> the least because of undue concentration by any
> one or any group on commercial and profit con-
> siderations. The game is on higher ground; it be-
> hooves every one to keep it there."

. . . . Trial . . . took place in May and June 1970. In an
ensuing opinion, Judge Cooper first noted that:

> "[Flood]'s witnesses in the main concede that
> some form of reserve on players is a necessary
> element of the organization of baseball as a
> league sport, but contend that the present all-
> embracing system is needlessly restrictive and of-
> fer various alternatives which in their   view

might loosen the bonds without sacrifice to the game. . . ."

He then held that *Federal Baseball Club v. National League* and *Toolson v. New York Yankees, Inc.* were controlling [set the standard for future cases] . . . and that judgment was to be entered for [Kuhn]. Judge Cooper included a statement of personal conviction to the effect that "negotiations could produce an accommodation on the reserve system which would be eminently fair and equitable to all concerned" and that "the reserve clause can be fashioned so as to find acceptance by player and club."

On appeal, the Second Circuit felt "compelled to affirm [uphold]." . . .

We granted certiorari [agreed to hear the case] in order to look once again at this troublesome and unusual situation.

Federal Baseball Club v. National League was a suit . . . instituted by a member of the Federal League (Baltimore) against the National and American Leagues and others. The plaintiff [Federal Baseball Club] obtained a verdict in the trial court, but the Court of Appeals reversed. The main brief filed by the [Federal Baseball Club] with this Court discloses that it was strenuously argued, among other things, that the business in which the defendants [the National and American Leagues] were engaged was interstate commerce; that the interstate relationship among the several clubs, located as they were in different States, was predominant; that organized baseball represented an investment of colossal wealth; that it was an engagement in moneymaking; that gate receipts were divided by agreement between the home club and the visiting club; and that the business of baseball was to be distinguished from the mere playing of the game as a sport for physical exercise and diversion.

Justice Holmes, in speaking succinctly for a unanimous Court said:

> "The business is giving exhibitions of baseball, which are purely state affairs. . . . But the fact that in order to give the exhibitions the Leagues must induce free persons to cross state lines and must arrange and pay for their doing so is not enough to change the character of the business. . . . [T]he transport is a mere incident, not the essential thing. That to which it is incident, the exhibition, although made for money would not be called trade or commerce in the commonly accepted use of those words. As it is put by the [National League], personal effort, not related to production, is not a subject of commerce. That which, in its consummation, is not commerce, does not become commerce among the states because the transportation that we have mentioned takes place. To repeat the illustrations given by the court below, a firm of lawyers sending out a member to argue a case, or the Chautauqua lecture bureau sending out lecturers, does not engage in such commerce because the lawyer or lecturer goes to another state.

> "If we are right, the [Federal Baseball Club]'s business is to be described in the same way; and the restrictions by contract that prevented the [Federal Baseball Club] from getting players to break their bargains, and the other conduct

charged against the [National League], were not
an interference with commerce among the states."

.... The only earlier case the parties were able to locate
where the question was raised whether organized baseball
was within the Sherman Act was *American League Baseball Club v. Chase*. That court had answered the question
in the negative.

Federal Baseball was cited a year later, and without disfa-
vor, in another opinion by Justice Holmes for a unanimous Court. ...

In the years that followed, baseball continued to be subject to intermittent antitrust attack. The courts, however,
rejected these challenges on the authority of *Federal Baseball*. In some cases stress was laid, although unsuccessfully, on new factors such as the development of radio and
television with their substantial additional revenues to
baseball. For the most part, however, the Holmes opinion
was generally and necessarily accepted as controlling authority. And in the 1952 Report of the Subcommittee on
Study of Monopoly Power of the House Committee on the
Judiciary, it was said, in conclusion:

"On the other hand the overwhelming preponderance of the evidence established baseball's need
for some sort of reserve clause. Baseball's history
shows that chaotic conditions prevailed when
there was no reserve clause. Experience points to
no feasible substitute to protect the integrity of
the game or to guarantee a comparatively even
competitive struggle. The evidence adduced
[given] at the hearings would clearly not justify

the enactment of legislation flatly condemning
the reserve clause."

.... [I]n the *Toolson, Kowalski,* and *Corbett* cases, ...
Federal Baseball was cited as holding "that the business of
providing public baseball games for profit between clubs
of professional baseball players was not within the scope
of the federal antitrust laws," and:

> "Congress has had the ruling under consideration
> but has not seen fit to bring such business under
> these laws by legislation having prospective ef-
> fect. The business has thus been left for thirty
> years to develop, on the understanding that it was
> not subject to existing antitrust legislation. The
> present cases ask us to overrule the prior decision
> and, with retrospective effect, hold the legislation
> applicable. We think that if there are evils in
> this field which now warrant application to it of
> the antitrust laws it should be by legislation. ...
> [T]he judgments [of the lower courts] are af-
> firmed on the authority of *Federal Baseball Club
> of Baltimore v. National League of Professional
> Baseball Clubs,* so far as that decision determines
> that Congress had no intention of including the
> business of baseball within the scope of the fed-
> eral antitrust laws."

.... Two Justices (Burton and Reed) dissented, stressing
the factual aspects, revenue sources, and the absence of an
express exemption of organized baseball from the Sherman Act. ...

It is of interest to note that in *Toolson* the petitioner had
argued flatly that *Federal Baseball* "is wrong and must be

overruled," and that Thomas Reed Powell, a constitutional scholar of no small stature, urged . . . that "baseball is a unique enterprise," and that "unbridled competition as applied to baseball would not be in the public interest."

United States v. Shubert was a civil antitrust action against defendants engaged in the production of legitimate theatrical attractions throughout the United States and in operating theaters for the presentation of such attractions. The District Court had dismissed the complaint on the authority of *Federal Baseball* and *Toolson.* This Court reversed. Chief Justice Warren noted the Court's broad conception of "trade or commerce" in the antitrust statutes and the types of enterprises already held to be within the reach of that phrase. He stated that *Federal Baseball* and *Toolson* afforded no basis for a conclusion that businesses built around the performance of local exhibitions are exempt from the antitrust laws. He then went on to elucidate the holding in *Toolson* by meticulously spelling out the factors mentioned above:

> "In *Federal Baseball,* the Court, speaking through Justice Holmes, was dealing with the business of baseball and nothing else. . . . The travel, the Court concluded, was 'a mere incident, not the essential thing.' . . .

> "In *Toolson,* where the issue was the same as in *Federal Baseball,* the Court was confronted with a unique combination of circumstances. For over 30 years there had stood a decision of this Court specifically fixing the status of the baseball business under the antitrust laws and more particularly the validity of the so-called 'reserve clause.' During this period, in reliance on the *Federal*

Baseball precedent, the baseball business had grown and developed. . . . And Congress, although it had actively considered the ruling, had not seen fit to reject it by amendatory legislation. Against this background, the Court in *Toolson* was asked to overrule *Federal Baseball* on the ground that it was out of step with subsequent decisions reflecting present-day concepts of interstate commerce. The Court, in view of the circumstances of the case, declined to do so. But neither did the Court necessarily reaffirm all that was said in *Federal Baseball*. Instead . . . the Court adhered to *Federal Baseball* 'so far as that decision determines that Congress had no intention of including the business of baseball within the scope of the federal antitrust laws.'. . ."

United States v. International Boxing Club was a companion to *Shubert* and was decided the same day. This was a civil antitrust action against defendants engaged in the business of promoting professional championship boxing contests. Here again the District Court had dismissed the complaint in reliance upon *Federal Baseball* and *Toolson*. The Chief Justice observed that "if it were not for *Federal Baseball* and *Toolson*, we think that it would be too clear for dispute that the Government's allegations bring the defendants within the scope of the Act." He pointed out that the defendants relied on the two baseball cases but also would have been content with a more restrictive interpretation of them than the *Shubert* defendants, for the boxing defendants argued that the cases immunized only businesses that involve exhibitions of an athletic nature. The Court accepted neither argument. It again noted that "*Toolson* neither overruled *Federal Baseball* nor necessarily reaffirmed all that was said in *Federal Baseball*."

. . . . The Court noted the presence then in Congress of various bills forbidding the application of the antitrust laws to "organized professional sports enterprises"; the holding of extensive hearings on some of these; subcommittee opposition; a postponement recommendation as to baseball; and the fact that "Congress thus left intact the then-existing coverage of the antitrust laws."

Justice Frankfurter, joined by Justice Minton, dissented. "It would baffle the subtlest ingenuity," he said, "to find a single differentiating factor between other sporting exhibitions . . . and baseball insofar as the conduct of the sport is relevant to the criteria or considerations by which the Sherman Law becomes applicable to a 'trade or commerce.'" . . .

Justice Minton also separately dissented on the ground that boxing is not trade or commerce. He added the comment that "Congress has not attempted" to control baseball and boxing. The two dissenting Justices, thus, did not call for the overruling of *Federal Baseball* and *Toolson;* they merely felt that boxing should be under the same umbrella of freedom as was baseball and, as Justice Frankfurter said, they could not exempt baseball "to the exclusion of every other sport different not one legal jot or tittle from it."

The parade marched on. *Radovich v. National Football League* was a civil Clayton Act case testing the application of the antitrust laws to professional football. The District Court dismissed. The Ninth Circuit affirmed in part on the basis of *Federal Baseball* and *Toolson.* The court did not hesitate to "confess that the strength of the pull" of the baseball cases and of *International Boxing* "is about equal," but then observed that "[f]ootball is a team sport" and boxing an individual one.

This Court reversed with an opinion by Justice Clark. He said that the Court made its ruling in *Toolson* "because it was concluded that more harm would be done in overruling *Federal Baseball* than in upholding a ruling which at best was of dubious validity." He noted that Congress had not acted. He then said:

> "All this, combined with the flood of litigation that would follow its repudiation, the harassment that would ensue, and the retroactive effect of such a decision, led the Court to the practical result that it should sustain [uphold] the unequivocal line of authority reaching over many years.

> "[S]ince *Toolson* and *Federal Baseball* are still cited as controlling authority in antitrust actions involving other fields of business, we now specifically limit the rule there established to the facts there involved, i.e., the business of organized professional baseball. As long as the Congress continues to acquiesce we should adhere to - but not extend - the interpretation of the Act made in those cases. . . .

> "If this ruling is unrealistic, inconsistent, or illogical, it is sufficient to answer, aside from the distinctions between the businesses, that were we considering the question of baseball for the first time upon a clean slate we would have no doubts. But *Federal Baseball* held the business of baseball outside the scope of the Act. No other business claiming the coverage of those cases has such an

adjudication [judgment]. We, therefore, conclude
that the orderly way to eliminate error or discrimination, if any there be, is by legislation and
not by court decision. . . ."

Justice Frankfurter dissented essentially for the reasons
stated in his dissent in *International Boxing.* Justice Harlan, joined by Justice Brennan, also dissented because he,
too, was "unable to distinguish football from baseball."
Here again the dissenting Justices did not call for the
overruling of the baseball decisions. They merely could
not distinguish the two sports and, out of respect for stare
decisis [the policy of standing by cases decided earlier],
voted to affirm.

Finally, in *Haywood v. National Basketball Association,*
Justice Douglas, in his capacity as Circuit Justice, reinstat-
ed a District Court's injunction [court order stopping an
action]. . . in favor of a professional basketball player and
said, "Basketball . . . does not enjoy exemption from the
antitrust laws."

This series of decisions understandably spawned extensive
commentary, some of it mildly critical and much of it not;
nearly all of it looked to Congress for any remedy that
might be deemed essential.

Legislative proposals have been numerous and persistent.
Since *Toolson* more than 50 bills have been introduced in
Congress relative to the applicability or nonapplicability
of the antitrust laws to baseball. A few of these passed
one house or the other. Those that did would have ex-
panded, not restricted, the reserve system's exemption to
other professional league sports. And the Act of September 30, 1961, and the merger addition thereto effected by

the Act of November 8, 1966, were also expansive rather than restrictive as to antitrust exemption.

In view of all this, it seems appropriate now to say that:

1. Professional baseball is a business and it is engaged in interstate commerce.

2. With its reserve system enjoying exemption from the federal antitrust laws, baseball is, in a very distinct sense, an exception and an anomaly. *Federal Baseball* and *Toolson* have become an aberration confined to baseball.

3. Even though others might regard this as "unrealistic, inconsistent, or illogical," the aberration is an established one, and one that has been recognized not only in *Federal Baseball* and *Toolson*, but in *Shubert, International Boxing*, and *Radovich*, as well, a total of five consecutive cases in this Court. It is an aberration that has been with us now for half a century, one heretofore deemed fully entitled to the benefit of stare decisis and one that has survived the Court's expanding concept of interstate commerce. It rests on a recognition and an acceptance of baseball's unique characteristics and needs.

4. Other professional sports operating interstate - football, boxing, basketball, and, presumably, hockey and golf - are not so exempt.

5. The advent of radio and television, with their consequent increased coverage and additional

revenues, has not occasioned an overruling of *Federal Baseball* and *Toolson.*

6. The Court has emphasized that since 1922 baseball, with full and continuing congressional awareness, has been allowed to develop and to expand unhindered by federal legislative action. Remedial legislation has been introduced repeatedly in Congress but none has ever been enacted. The Court, accordingly, has concluded that Congress as yet has had no intention to subject baseball's reserve system to the reach of the antitrust statutes. This, obviously, has been deemed to be something other than mere congressional silence and passivity.

7. The Court has expressed concern about the confusion and the retroactivity problems that inevitably would result with a judicial overturning of *Federal Baseball.* It has voiced a preference that if any change is to be made, it come by legislative action that, by its nature, is only prospective in operation.

8. The Court noted in *Radovich* that the slate with respect to baseball is not clean. Indeed, it has not been clean for half a century.

This emphasis and this concern are still with us. We continue to be loath, 50 years after *Federal Baseball* and almost two decades after *Toolson,* to overturn those cases judicially when Congress, by its positive inaction, has allowed those decisions to stand for so long and, far beyond mere infer-

ence and implication, has clearly evinced a desire
not to disapprove them legislatively.

Accordingly, we adhere once again to *Federal Baseball*
and *Toolson* and to their application to professional baseball. We adhere also to *International Boxing* and *Radovich* and to their respective applications to professional
boxing and professional football. If there is any inconsistency or illogic in all this, it is an inconsistency and illogic
of long standing that is to be remedied by the Congress
and not by this Court. If we were to act otherwise, we
would be withdrawing from the conclusion as to congressional intent made in *Toolson* and from the concerns as to
retrospectivity therein expressed. Under these circumstances, there is merit in consistency even though some
might claim that beneath that consistency is a layer of inconsistency.

. . . . The conclusion we have reached makes it unnecessary for us to consider [Kuhn]'s additional argument that
the reserve system is a mandatory subject of collective
bargaining and that federal labor policy therefore ex-
empts the reserve system from the operation of federal
antitrust laws.

We repeat for this case what was said in *Toolson*:

> "Without re-examination of the underlying issues,
> the [judgment] below [is] affirmed on the author-
> ity of *Federal Baseball Club of Baltimore v. Na-
> tional League of Professional Baseball Clubs*, so
> far as that decision determines that Congress had
> no intention of including the business of baseball
> within the scope of the federal antitrust laws."

And what the Court said in *Federal Baseball* in 1922 and what it said in *Toolson* in 1953, we say again here in 1972: the remedy, if any is indicated, is for congressional, and not judicial, action.

The judgment of the Court of Appeals is affirmed.

EQUAL PAY FOR EQUAL WORK

Corning v. Brennan

No employer shall discriminate between employees on the basis of sex by paying wages to employees at a rate less than the rate at which he pays wages to employees of the opposite sex for equal work on the jobs the performance of which requires equal skill, effort, and responsibility, and which are performed under similar working conditions.   **The Equal Pay Act of 1963**

The United States Congress passed the Equal Pay Act of 1963 to remedy the serious and pervasive problem of sexual wage discrimination in private industry. The guiding principle of the Equal Pay Act was simply: "Equal work will be rewarded by equal wages."

Women working in two Corning Glass Works plants, in New York and Pennsylvania, were, prior to the passage of the Equal Pay Act, paid significantly less for working on the day shift than males doing the exact same work, were paid working on the night shift. After passage of the Equal Pay Act, Corning Glass equalized the male-night, female-day wages, but initiated a new pay scale based on "job evaluation," which served to perpetuate the former sexual wage differences. U.S. Secretary of Labor Peter J. Brennan sued Corning Glass in both New York and Pennsylvania Federal District Courts for violating the Equal Pay Act. The New York District Court found for the women workers. The Pennsylvania District Court found for their employer. The U.S. Courts of Appeals for New York and Pennsylvania upheld the differing verdicts. Both sides appealed to the United States Supreme Court.

Associate Justice Thurgood Marshall delivered the 5-3 opinion (Justice Stewart did not participate) of the Court on June 3, 1974. The edited text follows.

THE CORNING COURT

Chief Justice Warren Burger
Appointed Chief Justice by President Nixon
Served 1969 - 1986

Associate Justice William O. Douglas
Appointed by President Franklin D. Roosevelt
Served 1939 - 1975

Associate Justice William Brennan
Appointed by President Eisenhower
Served 1956 - 1990

Associate Justice Byron White
Appointed by President Kennedy
Served 1962 - 1993

Associate Justice Thurgood Marshall
Appointed by President Lyndon Johnson
Served 1967 - 1991

Associate Justice Harry Blackmun
Appointed by President Nixon
Served 1970 - 1994

Associate Justice Lewis Powell
Appointed by President Nixon
Served 1971 - 1987

Associate Justice William Rehnquist
Appointed Associate Justice by President Nixon
Served 1971 -

The unedited text of *Corning v. Brennan* can be found
on page 188, volume 417 of *United States Reports.*

BRENNAN v. CORNING GLASS WORKS
JUNE 3, 1974

JUSTICE MARSHALL: These cases arise under the Equal Pay Act of 1963, which added to Section 6 of the Fair Labor Standards Act of 1938 the principle of equal pay for equal work regardless of sex. The principal question posed is whether Corning Glass Works violated the Act by paying a higher base wage to male night shift inspectors than it paid to female inspectors performing the same tasks on the day shift, where the higher wage was paid in addition to a separate night shift differential paid to all employees for night work. In [the New York case], the Court of Appeals for the Second Circuit, in a case involving several Corning plants in Corning, New York, held that this practice violated the Act. In [the Pennsylvania case], the Court of Appeals for the Third Circuit, in a case involving a Corning plant in Wellsboro, Pennsylvania, reached the opposite conclusion. We granted certiorari [agreed to hear] and consolidated the cases to resolve this unusually direct conflict between two circuits. Finding ourselves in substantial agreement with the analysis of the Second Circuit, we affirm [uphold] in [the New York case] and reverse in [the Pennsylvania case].

Prior to 1925, Corning operated its plants in Wellsboro and Corning only during the day, and all inspection work was performed by women. Between 1925 and 1930, the company began to introduce automatic production equipment which made it desirable to institute a night shift. During this period, however, both New York and Pennsylvania law prohibited women from working at night. As a result, in order to fill inspector positions on the new night shift, the company had to recruit male employees from among its male dayworkers. The male employees so trans-

ferred demanded and received wages substantially higher
than those paid to women inspectors engaged on the two
day shifts. During this same period, however, no plant-
wide shift differential existed and male employees working at night, other than inspectors, received the same
wages as their day shift counterparts. Thus a situation developed where the night inspectors were all male, the day
inspectors all female, and the male inspectors received significantly higher wages.

In 1944, Corning plants at both locations were organized
by a labor union and a collective-bargaining agreement
was negotiated for all production and maintenance employees. This agreement for the first time established a
plant-wide shift differential, but this change did not eliminate the higher base wage paid to male night inspectors.
Rather, the shift differential was superimposed on the existing difference in base wages between male night inspectors and female day inspectors.

Prior to June 11, 1964, the effective date of the Equal
Pay Act, the law in both Pennsylvania and New York was
amended to permit women to work at night. It was not
until some time after the effective date of the Act, however, that Corning initiated efforts to eliminate the differential rates for male and female inspectors. Beginning in
June 1966, Corning started to open up jobs on the night
shift to women. Previously separate male and female seniority lists were consolidated and women became eligible
to exercise their seniority, on the same basis as men, to bid
for the higher paid night inspection jobs as vacancies occurred.

On January 20, 1969, a new collective-bargaining agreement went into effect, establishing a new "job evaluation"

system for setting wage rates. The new agreement abolished for the future the separate base wages for day and night shift inspectors and imposed a uniform base wage for inspectors exceeding the wage rate for the night shift previously in effect. All inspectors hired after January 20, 1969, were to receive the same base wage, whatever their sex or shift. The collective-bargaining agreement further provided, however, for a higher "red circle" rate for employees hired prior to January 20, 1969, when working as inspectors on the night shift. This "red circle" rate served essentially to perpetuate the differential in base wages between day and night inspectors.

The Secretary of Labor brought these cases [to court] to enjoin [stop] Corning from violating the Equal Pay Act and to collect back wages allegedly due female employees because of past violations. Three distinct questions are presented: (1) Did Corning ever violate the Equal Pay Act by paying male night shift inspectors more than female day shift inspectors? (2) If so, did Corning cure its violation of the Act in 1966 by permitting women to work as night shift inspectors? (3) Finally, if the violation was not remedied in 1966, did Corning cure its violation in 1969 by equalizing day and night inspector wage rates but establishing higher "red circle" rates for existing employees working on the night shift?

Congress' purpose in enacting the Equal Pay Act was to remedy what was perceived to be a serious and endemic problem of employment discrimination in private industry - the fact that the wage structure of "many segments of American industry has been based on an ancient but outmoded belief that a man, because of his role in society, should be paid more than a woman even though his duties are the same." The solution adopted was quite simple in principle: to require that "equal work will be rewarded by equal wages."

The Act's basic structure and operation are similarly straightforward. In order to make out a case under the Act, the Secretary must show that an employer pays different wages to employees of opposite sexes "for equal work on jobs the performance of which requires equal skill, effort, and responsibility, and which are performed under similar working conditions." Although the Act is silent on this point, its legislative history makes plain that the Secretary has the burden of proof on this issue, as both of the [lower courts] recognized.

The Act also establishes four exceptions - three specific and one a catchall provision - where different payment to employees of opposite sexes "is made pursuant to (i) a seniority system; (ii) a merit system; (iii) a system which measures earnings by quantity or quality of production; or (iv) a differential based on any other factor other than sex." Again, while the Act is silent on this question, its structure and history also suggest that once the Secretary has carried his burden of showing that the employer pays workers of one sex more than workers of the opposite sex for equal work, the burden shifts to the employer to show that the differential is justified under one of the Act's four exceptions. All of the many lower courts that have considered this question have so held and this view is consistent with the general rule that the application of an exemption under the Fair Labor Standards Act is a matter of affirmative defense on which the employer has the burden of proof.

The contentions of the parties in this case reflect the Act's underlying framework. Corning argues that the

Secretary has failed to prove that Corning ever violated the Act because day shift work is not "performed under similar working conditions" as night shift work. The Secretary maintains that day shift and night shift work are performed under "similar working conditions" within the meaning of the Act. Although the Secretary recognizes that higher wages may be paid for night shift work, the Secretary contends that such a shift differential would be based upon a "factor other than sex" within the catch-all exception to the Act and that Corning has failed to carry its burden of proof that its higher base wage for male night inspectors was in fact based on any factor other than sex.

The [lower courts] relied in part on conflicting statements in the legislative history having some bearing on this question of statutory construction. The Third Circuit found particularly significant a statement of Congressman Goodell, a sponsor of the Equal Pay bill, who, in the course of explaining the bill on the floor of the House, commented that "standing as opposed to sitting, pleasantness or unpleasantness of surroundings, periodic rest periods, hours of work, *difference in shift*, all would logically fall within the working condition factor." The Second Circuit, in contrast, relied on a statement from the House Committee Report which, in describing the broad general exception for differentials "based on any other factor other than sex," stated: "Thus, among other things, shift differentials . . . would also be excluded. . . ."

We agree with Judge Friendly, however, that in this case a better understanding of the phrase "performed under similar working conditions" can be obtained from a consideration of the way in which Congress arrived at the statutory language than from trying to reconcile or estab-

lish preferences between the conflicting interpretations of
the Act by individual legislators or the committee reports.
As Justice Frankfurter remarked in an earlier case involving interpretation of the Fair Labor Standards Act,
"regard for the specific history of the legislative process
that culminated in the Act now before us affords more
solid ground for giving it appropriate meaning."

The most notable feature of the history of the Equal Pay
Act is that Congress recognized early in the legislative
process that the concept of equal pay for equal work was
more readily stated in principle than reduced to statutory
language which would be meaningful to employers and
workable across the broad range of industries covered by
the Act. As originally introduced, the Equal Pay bills required equal pay for "equal work on jobs the performance
of which requires equal skills." There were only two exceptions - for differentials "made pursuant to a seniority
or merit increase system which does not discriminate on
the basis of sex. . . ."

In both the House and Senate committee hearings, witnesses were highly critical of the Act's definition of equal
work and of its exemptions. Many noted that most of
American industry used formal, systematic job evaluation
plans to establish equitable wage structures in their plants.
Such systems, as explained coincidently by a representative of Corning Glass Works who testified at both hearings, took into consideration four separate factors in determining job value - skill, effort, responsibility and working conditions - and each of these four components was
further systematically divided into various subcomponents. Under a job evaluation plan, point values are assigned to each of the subcomponents of a given job, re-

sulting in a total point figure representing a relatively objective measure of the job's value.

In comparison to the rather complex job evaluation plans
used by industry, the definition of equal work used in the
first drafts of the Equal Pay Act was criticized as unduly
vague and incomplete. Industry representatives feared
that as a result of the Act's definition of equal work, the
Secretary of Labor would be cast in the position of
second-guessing the validity of a company's job evaluation
system. They repeatedly urged that the bill be amended
to include an exception for job classification systems, or
otherwise to incorporate the language of job evaluation
into the bill. Thus Corning's own representative testified:

> "Job evaluation is an accepted and tested method
> of attaining equity in wage relationship.

> "A great part of industry is committed to job
> evaluation by past practice and by contractual
> agreement as the basis for wage administration.

> "'Skill' alone, as a criterion, fails to recognize oth-
> er aspects of the job situation that affect job
> worth.

> "We sincerely hope that this committee in passing
> legislation to eliminate wage differences based on
> sex alone, will recognize in its language the gen-
> eral role of job evaluation in establishing equita-
> ble rate relationship."

We think it plain that in amending the Act's definition of
equal work to its present form, the Congress acted in di-

rect response to these pleas. Spokesmen for the amended
bill stated, for example, during the House debates:

> "The concept of equal pay for jobs demanding
> equal skill has been expanded to require also
> equal effort, responsibility, and similar working
> conditions. These factors are the core of all job
> classification systems. They form a legitimate ba-
> sis for differentials in pay."

Indeed, the most telling evidence of congressional intent is
the fact that the Act's amended definition of equal work
incorporated the specific language of the job evaluation
plan described at the hearings by Corning's own representative - that is, the concepts of "skill," "effort,"
"responsibility," and "working conditions."

Congress' intent, as manifested in this history, was to use
these terms to incorporate into the new federal act the
well-defined and well-accepted principles of job evaluation so as to ensure that wage differentials based upon
bona fide job evaluation plans would be outside the purview of the Act. The House Report emphasized:

> "This language recognizes that there are many
> factors which may be used to measure the rela-
> tionships between jobs and which establish a val-
> id basis for a difference in pay. These factors
> will be found in a majority of the job classifica-
> tion systems. Thus, it is anticipated that a bona
> fide job classification program that does not dis-
> criminate on the basis of sex will serve as a valid
> defense to a charge of discrimination."

It is in this light that the phrase "working conditions" must be understood, for where Congress has used technical words or terms of art, "it [is] proper to explain them by reference to the art or science to which they [are] appropriate." This principle is particularly salutary where, as here, the legislative history reveals that Congress incorporated words having a special meaning within the field regulated by the statute so as to overcome objections by industry representatives that statutory definitions were vague and incomplete.

While a layman might well assume that time of day worked reflects one aspect of a job's "working conditions," the term has a different and much more specific meaning in the language of industrial relations. As Corning's own representative testified at the hearings, the element of working conditions encompasses two subfactors: "surroundings" and "hazards." "Surroundings" measures the elements, such as toxic chemicals or fumes, regularly encountered by a worker, their intensity, and their frequency. "Hazards" takes into account the physical hazards regularly encountered, their frequency, and the severity of injury they can cause. This definition of "working conditions" is not only manifested in Corning's own job evaluation plans but is also well accepted across a wide range of American industry.

Nowhere in any of these definitions is time of day worked mentioned as a relevant criterion. The fact of the matter is that the concept of "working conditions," as used in the specialized language of job evaluation systems, simply does not encompass shift differentials. Indeed, while Corning now argues that night inspection work is not equal to day inspection work, all of its own job evaluation plans, including the one now in effect, have consistently treated them as equal in all respects, including working conditions. And Corning's Manager of Job Evaluation testified in [the New York case] that time of day worked was not considered to be a "working condition." Significantly, it is not the Secretary in this case who is trying to look behind Corning's bona fide job evaluation system to require equal pay for jobs which Corning has historically viewed as unequal work. Rather, it is Corning which asks us to differentiate between jobs which the company itself has always equated. We agree with the Second Circuit that the inspection work at issue in this case, whether performed during the day or night, is "equal work" as that term is defined in the Act.

This does not mean, of course, that there is no room in the Equal Pay Act for nondiscriminatory shift differentials. Work on a steady night shift no doubt has psychological and physiological impacts making it less attractive than work on a day shift. The Act contemplates that a male night worker may receive a higher wage than a female day worker, just as it contemplates that a male employee with 20 years' seniority can receive a higher wage than a woman with two years seniority. Factors such as these play a role under the Act's four exceptions - the seniority differential under the specific seniority exception, the shift differential under the catch-all exception for differentials "based on any other factor other than sex."

The question remains, however, whether Corning carried its burden of proving that the higher rate paid for night inspection work, until 1966 performed solely by men, was in fact intended to serve as compensation for night work, or rather constituted an added payment based upon sex. We agree that the record amply supports the District Court's conclusion that Corning had not sustained [upheld] its burden of proof. As its history revealed, "the higher night rate was in large part the product of the generally higher wage level of male workers and the need to compensate them for performing what were regarded as demeaning tasks." The differential in base wages originated at a time when no other night employees received higher pay than corresponding day workers and it was maintained long after the company instituted a separate plant-wide shift differential which was thought to compensate adequately for the additional burdens of night work. The differential arose simply because men would not work at the low rates paid women inspectors, and it reflected a job market in which Corning could pay women less than men for the same work. That the company took advantage of such a situation may be understandable as a matter of economics, but its differential nevertheless became illegal once Congress enacted into law the principle of equal pay for equal work.

We now must consider whether Corning continued to remain in violation of the Act after 1966 when, without changing the base wage rates for day and night inspectors, it began to permit women to bid for jobs on the night shift as vacancies occurred. It is evident that this was more than a token gesture to end discrimination, as turnover in the night shift inspection jobs was rapid. The record in [the New York case] shows, for example, that during the two-year period after June 1, 1966, the date women were first permitted to bid for night inspection jobs, women took 152 of the 278 openings, and women with very little seniority were able to obtain positions on the night shift. Relying on these facts, the company argues that it ceased discriminating against women in 1966, and was no longer in violation of the Equal Pay Act.

But the issue before us is not whether the company, in some abstract sense, can be said to have treated men the same as women after 1966. Rather, the question is whether the company remedied the specific violation of the Act which the Secretary proved. We agree with the Second Circuit, as well as with all other circuits that have had occasion to consider this issue, that the company could not cure its violation except by equalizing the base wages of female day inspectors with the higher rates paid the night inspectors. This result is implicit in the Act's language, its statement of purpose, and its legislative history.

As the Second Circuit noted, Congress enacted the Equal Pay Act "[r]ecognizing the weaker bargaining position of many women and believing that discrimination in wage rates represented unfair employer exploitation of this source of cheap labor." In response to evidence of the many families dependent on the income of working women, Congress included in the Act's statement of purpose a finding that "the existence . . . of wage differentials based on sex . . . depresses wages and living standards for employees necessary for their health and efficiency." And Congress declared it to be the policy of the Act to correct this condition.

To achieve this end, Congress required that employers pay equal pay for equal work and then specified:

> *"Provided,* That an employer who is paying a wage rate differential in violation of this subsection shall not, in order to comply with the provisions of this subsection, reduce the wage rate of any employee."

The purpose of this proviso was to ensure that to remedy violations of the Act, "[t]he lower wage rate must be increased to the level of the higher." Comments of individual legislators are all consistent with this view. Representative Dwyer remarked, for example, "The objective of equal pay legislation . . . is not to drag down men workers to the wage levels of women, but to raise women to the levels enjoyed by men in cases were discrimination is still practiced." Representative Griffin also thought it clear that "[t]he only way a violation could be remedied under the bill . . . is for the lower wages to be raised to the higher."

By proving that after the effective date of the Equal Pay Act, Corning paid female day inspectors less than male night inspectors for equal work, the Secretary implicitly demonstrated that the wages of female day shift inspectors were unlawfully depressed and that the fair wage for inspection work was the base wage paid to male inspectors on the night shift. The whole purpose of the Act was to require that these depressed wages be raised, in part as a matter of simple justice to the employees themselves, but also as a matter of market economics, since Congress recognized as well that discrimination in wages on the basis of sex "constitutes an unfair method of competition."

We agree with Judge Friendly that

> "In light of this apparent congressional understanding, we cannot hold that Corning, by allowing some - or even many - women to move into the higher paid night jobs, achieved full compliance with the Act. Corning's action still left the inspectors on the day shift - virtually all women - earning a lower base wage than the night shift in-

spectors because of a differential initially based
on sex and still not justified by any other consideration; in effect, Corning was still taking advantage of the availability of female labor to fill its
day shift at a differentially low wage rate not
justified by any factor other than sex."

The Equal Pay Act is broadly remedial, and it should be
construed [interpreted] and applied so as to fulfill the underlying purposes which Congress sought to achieve. If,
as the Secretary proved, the work performed by women
on the day shift was equal to that performed by men on
the night shift, the company became obligated to pay the
women the same base wage as their male counterparts on
the effective date of the Act. To permit the company to
escape that obligation by agreeing to allow some women
to work on the night shift at a higher rate of pay as vacancies occurred would frustrate, not serve, Congress'
ends.

The company's final contention - that it cured its violation of the Act when a new collective-bargaining agreement went into effect on January 20, 1969 - need not de-
tain us long. While the new agreement provided for equal
base wages for night or day inspectors hired after that
date, it continued to provide unequal base wages for employees hired before that date, a discrimination likely to
continue for some time into the future because of a large
number of laid-off employees who had to be offered re-
employment before new inspectors could be hired. After
considering the rather complex method in which the new
wage rates for employees hired prior to January 1969
were calculated and the company's stated purpose behind
the provisions of the new agreement, the District Court in
[the New York case] concluded that the lower base-wage

for day inspectors was a direct product of the company's failure to equalize the base wages for male and female inspectors as of the effective date of the Act. We agree it is clear from the record that had the company equalized the base wage rates of male and female inspectors on the effective date of the Act, as the law required, the day inspectors in 1969 would have been entitled to the same higher "red circle" rate the company provided for night inspectors. We therefore conclude that . . . the company's continued discrimination in base wages between night and day workers, though phrased in terms of a neutral factor other than sex, nevertheless operated to perpetuate the effects of the company's prior illegal practice of paying women less than men for equal work.

The judgment in [the New York case] is affirmed. The judgment in [the Pennsylvania case] is reversed and the case remanded [sent back] to the Court of Appeals for further proceedings consistent with this opinion.

It is so ordered.

CHILD ABUSE

DeShaney v. Winnebago County Department of Social Services

"I just knew the phone would ring some day and Joshua would be dead." - **Winnebago County Social Worker**

In March 1984 Joshua DeShaney, four years old, was so severely beaten by his father that he suffered irreversible brain damage and was expected to spend the rest of his life in an institution for the profoundly retarded. The father, Randy DeShaney, was convicted of child abuse.

The DeShaneys, father and son, moved to Neenah, a city in Winnebago County, Wisconsin, in 1980, shortly after Randy DeShaney's divorce from Joshua's mother Melody. In January 1982 the Winnebago County Department of Social Services began to receive reports from family, neighbors, and the local hospital that Joshua was being abused. Randy DeShaney denied abusing Joshua. After continued abuse reports Joshua was taken away from his father. Winnebago County's Child Protection Team, a pediatrician, a psychologist, a police detective, a lawyer, several social service workers, and hospital personnel, decided that there was insufficient evidence that Randy was abusing Joshua and returned the boy to his father. Child abuse incidents continued to be reported, with no governmental intervention, until Joshua's near-death.

Melody DeShaney sued the Winnebago Department of Social Services in a U.S. District Court, charging that their failure to intervene to stop the abuse denied Joshua of his liberty without due process of law, a violation of the Fourteenth Amendment. The District Court found against the DeShaneys, as did the U.S. Court of Appeals. The DeShaneys appealed to the United States Supreme Court.

Chief Justice William Rehnquist delivered the Court's 6-3 opinion on February 22, 1989. The edited text follows.

THE DeSHANEY COURT

Chief Justice William Rehnquist
Appointed Chief Justice by President Reagan
Appointed Associate Justice by President Nixon
Served 1971 -

Associate Justice William Brennan
Appointed by President Eisenhower
Served 1956 - 1990

Associate Justice Byron White
Appointed by President Kennedy
Served 1962 - 1993

Associate Justice Thurgood Marshall
Appointed by President Lyndon Johnson
Served 1967 - 1991

Associate Justice Harry Blackmun
Appointed by President Nixon
Served 1970 - 1994

Associate Justice John Paul Stevens
Appointed by President Ford
Served 1975 -

Associate Justice Sandra Day O'Connor
Appointed Chief Justice by President Reagan
Served 1981 -

Associate Justice Antonin Scalia
Appointed by President Reagan
Served 1986 -

Associate Justice Anthony Kennedy
Appointed by President Reagan
Served 1988 -

The unedited text of *DeShaney v. Winnebago County Department of Social Services* can be found in volume 417 of *United States Reports*.

DeSHANEY v.
WINNEBAGO COUNTY SOCIAL SERVICES
FEBRUARY 22, 1989

CHIEF JUSTICE REHNQUIST: Petitioner [Joshua De-
Shaney] is a boy who was beaten and permanently injured
by his father, with whom he lived. The respondents
[Winnebago County Department of Social Services (DSS)]
are social workers and other local officials who received
complaints that [Joshua] was being abused by his father
and had reason to believe that this was the case, but no-
netheless did not act to remove [him] from his father's
custody. [Joshua] sued [DSS] claiming that their failure
to act deprived him of his liberty in violation of the Due
Process Clause of the Fourteenth Amendment to the United States Constitution. We hold that it did not.

The facts of this case are undeniably tragic. Petitioner
Joshua DeShaney was born in 1979. In 1980, a Wyoming
court granted his parents a divorce and awarded custody
of Joshua to his father, Randy DeShaney. The father
shortly thereafter moved to Neenah, a city located in Winnebago County, Wisconsin, taking the infant Joshua with
him. There he entered into a second marriage, which also
ended in divorce.

The Winnebago County authorities first learned that Joshua DeShaney might be a victim of child abuse in January
1982, when his father's second wife complained to the police, at the time of their divorce, that he had previously
"hit the boy causing marks and [was] a prime case for
child abuse." The Winnebago County Department of Social Services (DSS) interviewed the father, but he denied
the accusations, and DSS did not pursue them further. In

January 1983, Joshua was admitted to a local hospital with multiple bruises and abrasions. The examining physician suspected child abuse and notified DSS, which immediately obtained an order from a Wisconsin juvenile court placing Joshua in the temporary custody of the hospital. Three days later, the county convened [a] "Child Protection Team" - consisting of a pediatrician, a psychologist, a police detective, the county's lawyer, several DSS caseworkers, and various hospital personnel - to consider Joshua's situation. At this meeting, the Team decided that there was insufficient evidence of child abuse to retain Joshua in the custody of the court. The Team did, however, decide to recommend several measures to protect Joshua, including enrolling him in a preschool program, providing his father with certain counselling services, and encouraging his father's girlfriend to move out of the home. Randy DeShaney entered into a voluntary agreement with DSS in which he promised to cooperate with them in accomplishing these goals.

Based on the recommendation of the Child Protection Team, the juvenile court dismissed the child protection case and returned Joshua to the custody of his father. A month later, emergency room personnel called the DSS caseworker handling Joshua's case to report that he had once again been treated for suspicious injuries. The caseworker concluded that there was no basis for action. For the next six months, the caseworker made monthly visits to the DeShaney home, during which she observed a number of suspicious injuries on Joshua's head; she also noticed that he had not been enrolled in school and that the girlfriend had not moved out. The caseworker dutifully recorded these incidents in her files, along with her continuing suspicions that someone in the DeShaney household was physically abusing Joshua, but she did nothing more. In November 1983, the emergency room notified DSS that Joshua had been treated once again for injuries that they believed to be caused by child abuse. On the caseworker's next two visits to the DeShaney home, she was told that Joshua was too ill to see her. Still DSS took no action.

In March 1984, Randy DeShaney beat 4-year-old Joshua so severely that he fell into a life-threatening coma. Emergency brain surgery revealed a series of hemorrhages caused by traumatic injuries to the head inflicted over a long period of time. Joshua did not die, but he suffered brain damage so severe that he is expected to spend the rest of his life confined to an institution for the profoundly retarded. Randy DeShaney was subsequently tried and convicted of child abuse.

Joshua and his mother brought this action . . . in the United States District Court for the Eastern District of Wisconsin against respondents Winnebago County, its Department of Social Services, and various individual employees of the Department. The complaint alleged [charged] that [DSS] had deprived Joshua of his liberty without due process of law, in violation of his rights under the Fourteenth Amendment, by failing to intervene to protect him against a risk of violence at his father's hands of which they knew or should have known. The District Court [found] for [DSS].

The Court of Appeals for the Seventh Circuit affirmed [upheld]. . . . First, the court held that the Due Process Clause of the Fourteenth Amendment does not require a state or local governmental entity to protect its citizens from "private violence, or other mishaps not attributable to the conduct of its employees." In so holding, the court specifically rejected the position . . . that once the State learns that a particular child is in danger of abuse from third parties and actually undertakes to protect him from that danger, a "special relationship" arises between it and the child which imposes an affirmative constitutional duty to provide adequate protection. Second, the court held . . . that the causal connection between [DSS]'s conduct and Joshua's injuries was too attenuated to establish a deprivation of constitutional rights. . . . The court therefore found it unnecessary to reach the question whether [DSS]'s conduct evinced the "state of mind" necessary to make out a due process claim. . . .

Because of the inconsistent approaches taken by the lower courts in determining when, if ever, the failure of a state or local governmental entity or its agents to provide an individual with adequate protective services constitutes a violation of the individual's due process rights, and the importance of the issue to the administration of state and local governments, we granted certiorari [agreed to hear the case]. We now affirm.

The Due Process Clause of the Fourteenth Amendment provides that "[n]o State shall . . . deprive any person of life, liberty, or property, without due process of law." [Joshua] contend[s] that the State deprived [him] of his liberty interest in "free[dom] from . . . unjustified intrusions on personal security" by failing to provide him with adequate protection against his father's violence. . . . [Joshua does] not claim that the State denied [him] protection without according him appropriate procedural safeguards, but that it was categorically obligated to protect him in these circumstances.

But nothing in the language of the Due Process Clause itself requires the State to protect the life, liberty, and property of its citizens against invasion by private actors. The Clause is phrased as a limitation on the State's power to act, not as a guarantee of certain minimal levels of safety and security. It forbids the State itself to deprive individuals of life, liberty, or property without "due process of law," but its language cannot fairly be extended to impose an affirmative obligation on the State to ensure that those interests do not come to harm through other means. Nor does history support such an expansive reading of the constitutional text. Like its counterpart in the Fifth Amendment, the Due Process Clause of the Fourteenth Amendment was intended to prevent government "from abusing [its] power, or employing it as an instrument of oppression." Its purpose was to protect the people from the State, not to ensure that the State protected them from each other. The Framers were content to leave the extent of governmental obligation in the latter area to the democratic political processes.

Consistent with these principles, our cases have recognized that the Due Process Clauses generally confer no affirmative right to governmental aid, even where such aid may be necessary to secure life, liberty, or property interests of which the government itself may not deprive the individual. As we said in *Harris v. McRae*, "[a]lthough the liberty protected by the Due Process Clause affords protection against unwarranted *government* interference . . . , it does not confer an entitlement to such [governmental aid] as may be necessary to realize all the advantages of that freedom." If the Due Process Clause does not require the State to provide its citizens with particular protective services, it follows that the State cannot be held liable under the Clause for injuries that could have been averted had it chosen to provide them. As a general matter, then, we conclude that a State's failure to protect an individual against private violence simply does not constitute a violation of the Due Process Clause.

[The DeShaneys] contend, however, that even if the Due Process Clause imposes no affirmative obligation on the State to provide the general public with adequate protective services, such a duty may arise out of certain "special relationships" created or assumed by the State with respect to particular individuals. [They] argue that such a "special relationship" existed here because the State knew that Joshua faced a special danger of abuse at his father's hands, and specifically proclaimed, by word and by deed, its intention to protect him against that danger. Having actually undertaken to protect Joshua from this danger - which [the DeShaneys] concede the State played no part in creating - the State acquired an affirmative "duty," enforceable through the Due Process Clause, to do so in a reasonably competent fashion. Its failure to discharge that duty, so the argument goes, was an abuse of governmental power that so "shocks the conscience" as to constitute a substantive due process violation.

We reject this argument. It is true that in certain limited circumstances the Constitution imposes upon the State affirmative duties of care and protection with respect to particular individuals. In *Estelle v. Gamble*, we recognized that the Eighth Amendment's prohibition against cruel and unusual punishment, made applicable to the States through the Fourteenth Amendment's Due Process Clause, requires the State to provide adequate medical care to incarcerated prisoners. We reasoned that because the prisoner is unable "'by reason of the deprivation of

his liberty [to] care for himself,'" it is only "'just'" that
the State be required to care for him.

In *Youngberg v. Romeo,* we extended this analysis beyond
the Eighth Amendment setting, holding that the substantive component of the Fourteenth Amendment's Due
Process Clause requires the State to provide involuntarily
committed mental patients with such services as are necessary to ensure their "reasonable safety" from themselves
and others. As we explained, "[i]f it is cruel and unusual
punishment to hold convicted criminals in unsafe conditions, it must be unconstitutional [under the Due Process
Clause] to confine the involuntarily committed - who may
not be punished at all - in unsafe conditions."

But these cases afford [Joshua] no help. Taken together,
they stand only for the proposition that when the State
takes a person into its custody and holds him there against
his will, the Constitution imposes upon it a corresponding
duty to assume some responsibility for his safety and general well-being. The rationale for this principle is simple
enough: when the State by the affirmative exercise of its
power so restrains an individual's liberty that it renders
him unable to care for himself, and at the same time fails
to provide for his basic human needs - e.g., food, clothing,
shelter, medical care, and reasonable safety - it transgresses the substantive limits on state action set by the Eighth
Amendment and the Due Process Clause. The affirmative
duty to protect arises not from the State's knowledge of
the individual's predicament or from its expressions of intent to help him, but from the limitation which it has imposed on his freedom to act on his own behalf. In the
substantive due process analysis, it is the State's affirmative act of restraining the individual's freedom to act on
his own behalf - through incarceration, institutionaliza-

tion, or other similar restraint of personal liberty - which is the "deprivation of liberty" triggering the protections of the Due Process Clause, not its failure to act to protect his liberty interests against harms inflicted by other means.

The *Estelle-Youngberg* analysis simply has no applicability in the present case. [The DeShaneys] concede that the harms Joshua suffered did not occur while he was in the State's custody, but while he was in the custody of his natural father, who was in no sense a state actor. While the State may have been aware of the dangers that Joshua faced in the free world, it played no part in their creation, nor did it do anything to render him any more vulnerable to them. That the State once took temporary custody of Joshua does not alter the analysis, for when it returned him to his father's custody, it placed him in no worse position than that in which he would have been had it not acted at all; the State does not become the permanent guarantor of an individual's safety by having once offered him shelter. Under these circumstances, the State had no constitutional duty to protect Joshua.

It may well be that, by voluntarily undertaking to protect Joshua against a danger it concededly played no part in creating, the State acquired a duty under state . . . law to provide him with adequate protection against that danger. But the claim here is based on the Due Process Clause of the Fourteenth Amendment, which, as we have said many times, does not transform every [injury] committed by a state actor into a constitutional violation. A State may, through its courts and legislatures, impose such affirmative duties of care and protection upon its agents as it wishes. But not "all common-law duties owed by government actors were . . . constitutionalized by the Fourteenth Amendment." Because, as explained above, the State had no constitutional duty to protect Joshua against his father's violence, its failure to do so - though calamitous in hindsight - simply does not constitute a violation of the Due Process Clause.

Judges and lawyers, like other humans, are moved by natural sympathy in a case like this to find a way for Joshua and his mother to receive adequate compensation for the grievous harm inflicted upon them. But before yielding to that impulse, it is well to remember once again that the harm was inflicted not by the State of Wisconsin, but by Joshua's father. The most that can be said of the state functionaries in this case is that they stood by and did nothing when suspicious circumstances dictated a more active role for them. In defense of them it must also be said that had they moved too soon to take custody of the son away from the father, they would likely have been met with charges of improperly intruding into the parent-child relationship, charges based on the same Due Process Clause that forms the basis for the present charge of failure to provide adequate protection.

The people of Wisconsin may well prefer a system of liability which would place upon the State and its officials the responsibility for failure to act in situations such as the present one. They may create such a system, if they do not have it already, by changing the . . . law of the State in accordance with the regular law-making process. But they should not have it thrust upon them by this Court's expansion of the Due Process Clause of the Fourteenth Amendment.

Affirmed.

THE "SON OF SAM" LAW

Simon & Schuster v. The New York State Crime Victims Board

[Every person or organization] contracting with any person accused or convicted of a crime, with respect to the reenactment of such crime, by way of a movie, book, magazine article, radio or television presentation, or from the expression of such person's thoughts, opinions, feelings or emotions about such crime, shall pay over [all profits to the Crime Victims Board].

New York State's "Son of Sam" Law

David Berkowitz, the "Son of Sam," terrorized New York City with a series of murders in the summer of 1974. The New York State Legislature soon after enacted the "Son of Sam" law to prevent persons accused or convicted of crimes from profiting from the sale of their life story. New York's "Son of Sam" law was never invoked against Berkowitz, who voluntary paid the proceeds from the sale of his life story to the families of his victims. The law was invoked by the Crime Victims Board in the cases of Jean Harris, convicted killer of the "Scarsdale Diet" Doctor, and Mark David Chapman, convicted killer of John Lennon.

Wiseguy, a bestseller [and basis for the movie *Goodfellas*] is the life story of mobster Henry Hill. New York's Crime Victims Board invoked the "Son of Sam" law against *Wiseguy* and ordered the publisher, Simon & Schuster, to pay over Hill's profits to his victims. The publisher sued the Board in U.S. District Court, asserting that the "Son of Sam" law was a violation of Hill's First Amendment rights. The District Court upheld the law, as did the Court of Appeals. Simon & Schuster appealed to the U.S. Supreme Court.

Associate Justice Sandra Day O'Connor delivered the Court's 8-0 (Justice Thomas did not participate) opinion on December 10, 1991. The edited text follows.

THE "SON OF SAM" LAW COURT

Chief Justice William Rehnquist
Appointed Chief Justice by President Reagan
Appointed Associate Justice by President Nixon
Served 1971 -

Associate Justice Byron White
Appointed by President Kennedy
Served 1962 - 1993

Associate Justice Harry Blackmun
Appointed by President Nixon
Served 1970 - 1994

Associate Justice John Paul Stevens
Appointed by President Ford
Served 1975 -

Associate Justice Sandra Day O'Connor
Appointed Chief Justice by President Reagan
Served 1981 -

Associate Justice Antonin Scalia
Appointed by President Reagan
Served 1986 -

Associate Justice Anthony Kennedy
Appointed by President Reagan
Served 1988 -

Associate Justice David Souter
Appointed by President Bush
Served 1990 -

The unedited text of *Simon & Schuster v. New York State Crime Victims Board* can be found on page 105, volume 502 of *United States Reports.*

SIMON & SCHUSTER v. NEW YORK STATE CRIME VICTIMS BOARD
DECEMBER 10, 1991

JUSTICE O'CONNOR: New York's "Son of Sam" law requires that an accused or convicted criminal's income from works describing his crime be deposited in an escrow account. These funds are then made available to the victims of the crime and the criminal's other creditors. We consider whether this statute is consistent with the First Amendment.

In the summer of 1977, New York was terrorized by a serial killer popularly known as the Son of Sam. The hunt for the Son of Sam received considerable publicity, and by the time David Berkowitz was identified as the killer and apprehended, the rights to his story were worth a substantial amount. Berkowitz's chance to profit from his notoriety while his victims and their families remained uncompensated did not escape the notice of New York's Legislature. The State quickly enacted the statute at issue.

The statute was intended to "ensure that monies received by the criminal under such circumstances shall first be made available to recompense the victims of that crime for their loss and suffering." As the author of the statute explained, "[i]t is abhorrent to one's sense of justice and decency that an individual . . . can expect to receive large sums of money for his story once he is captured - while five people are dead, [and] other people were injured as a result of his conduct."

The *Son of Sam* law, as later amended, requires any entity contracting with an accused or convicted person for a depiction of the crime to submit a copy of the contract to respondent Crime Victims Board, and to turn over any income under that contract to the Board. This requirement applies to all such contracts in any medium of communication:

> "Every person, firm, corporation, partnership, association or other legal entity contracting with any person or the representative or assignee of any person, accused or convicted of a crime in this state, with respect to the reenactment of such crime, by way of a movie, book, magazine article, tape recording, phonograph record, radio or television presentation, live entertainment of any kind, or from the expression of such accused or convicted person's thoughts, feelings, opinions or emotions regarding such crime, shall submit a copy of such contract to the board and pay over to the board any moneys which would otherwise, by terms of such contract, be owing to the person so accused or convicted or his representatives."

The Board is then required to deposit the payment in an escrow account "for the benefit of and payable to any victim . . . provided that such victim, within five years of the date of the establishment of such escrow account, brings a civil action in a court of competent jurisdiction and recovers a money judgment for damages against such [accused or convicted] person or his representatives." After five years, if no actions are pending, "the board shall immediately pay over any moneys in the escrow account to such person or his legal representatives." This 5-year period in which to bring a civil action against the convicted person begins to run when the escrow account is established, and supersedes any limitations period that expires earlier.

Subsection (8) grants priority to two classes of claims against the escrow account. First, upon a court order, the Board must release assets "for the exclusive purpose of retaining legal representation." In addition, the Board has the discretion, after giving notice to the victims of the crime, to "make payments from the escrow account to a representative of any person accused or convicted of a crime for the necessary expenses of the production of the moneys paid into the escrow account." This provision permits payments to literary agents and other such representatives. Payments under subsection (8) may not exceed one-fifth of the amount collected in the account.

Claims against the account are given the following priorities: (a) payments ordered by the Board under subsection (8); (b) subrogation [third party] claims of the State for payments made to victims of the crime; (c) civil judgments obtained by victims of the crime; and (d) claims of other creditors of the accused or convicted person, including state and local tax authorities.

Subsection (10) broadly defines "person convicted of a crime" to include "any person convicted of a crime in this state either by entry of a plea of guilty or by conviction after trial *and any person who has voluntarily and intelligently admitted the commission of a crime for which such person is not prosecuted.*" Thus a person who has never been accused or convicted of a crime in the ordinary sense, but who admits in a book or other work to having committed a crime, is within the statute's coverage.

As recently construed [interpreted] by the New York Court of Appeals, however, the statute does not apply to victimless crimes.

The *Son of Sam* law supplements pre-existing statutory schemes authorizing the Board to compensate crime victims for their losses, permitting courts to order the proceeds of crime forfeited to the State, providing for orders of restitution at sentencing, and affording prejudgment attachment procedures to ensure that wrongdoers do not dissipate their assets. The escrow arrangement established by the *Son of Sam* law enhances these provisions only insofar as the accused or convicted person earns income within the scope of Section 632-a(1).

Since its enactment in 1977, the *Son of Sam* law has been invoked only a handful of times. As might be expected, the individuals whose profits the Board has sought to escrow have all become well known for having committed highly publicized crimes. These include Jean Harris, the convicted killer of "Scarsdale Diet" Doctor Herman Tarnower; Mark David Chapman, the man convicted of assassinating John Lennon; and R. Foster Winans, the former Wall Street Journal columnist convicted of insider trading. Ironically, the statute was never applied to the Son of Sam himself; David Berkowitz was found incompetent to stand trial, and the statute at that time applied only to criminals who had actually been convicted. According to the Board, Berkowitz voluntarily paid his share of the royalties from the book *Son of Sam*, published in 1981, to his victims or their estates.

This case began in 1986, when the Board first became aware of the contract between petitioner Simon & Schuster and admitted organized crime figure Henry Hill.

Looking back from the safety of the Federal Witness Protection Program, Henry Hill recalled: "At the age of twelve my ambition was to be a gangster. To be a wiseguy. To me being a wiseguy was better than being president of the United States." Whatever one might think of Hill, at the very least it can be said that he realized his dreams. After a career spanning 25 years, Hill admitted engineering some of the most daring crimes of his day, including the 1978-1979 Boston College basketball point-shaving scandal, and the theft of $6 million from Lufthansa Airlines in 1978, the largest successful cash robbery in American history. Most of Hill's crimes were more banausic: He committed extortion, he imported and distributed narcotics, and he organized numerous robberies.

Hill was arrested in 1980. In exchange for immunity from prosecution, he testified against many of his former colleagues. Since his arrest, he has lived under an assumed name in an unknown part of the country.

In August 1981, Hill entered into a contract with author Nicholas Pileggi for the production of a book about Hill's life. The following month, Hill and Pileggi signed a publishing agreement with Simon & Schuster. Under the agreement, Simon & Schuster agreed to make payments to both Hill and Pileggi. Over the next few years, according to Pileggi, he and Hill "talked at length virtually every single day, with not more than an occasional Sunday or holiday skipped. We spent more than three hundred hours together; my notes of conversations with Henry occupy more than six linear file feet." Because producing the book required such a substantial investment of time and effort, Hill sought compensation.

The result of Hill and Pileggi's collaboration was *Wiseguy*, which was published in January 1986. The book depicts, in colorful detail, the day-to-day existence of organized crime, primarily in Hill's first-person narrative.

Throughout *Wiseguy*, Hill frankly admits to having participated in an astonishing variety of crimes. He discusses, among other things, his conviction of extortion and the prison sentence he served. In one portion of the book, Hill recounts how members of the Mafia received preferential treatment in prison:

"The dorm was a separate three-story building outside the wall, which looked more like a Holiday Inn than a prison. There were four guys to a room, and we had comfortable beds and private baths. There were two dozen rooms on each floor, and each of them had mob guys living in them. It was like a wiseguy convention - the whole Gotti crew, Jimmy Doyle and his guys, 'Ernie Boy' Abbamonte and 'Joe Crow' Delvecchio, Vinnie Aloi, Frank Cotroni.

"It was wild. There was wine and booze, and it was kept in bath-oil or after-shave jars. The hacks in the honor dorm were almost all on the take, and even though it was against the rules, we used to cook in our rooms. Looking back, I don't think Paulie went to the general mess five times in the two and a half years he was there. We had a stove and pots and pans and silverware stacked in the bathroom. We had glasses and an ice-water cooler where we kept the fresh meats and cheeses. When there was an inspection, we stored the stuff in the false ceiling, and once in a while, if it was confiscated, we'd just go to the kitchen and get new stuff.

"We had the best food smuggled into our dorm from the kitchen. Steaks, veal cutlets, shrimp, red snapper. Whatever the hacks could buy, we ate. It cost me two, three hundred a week. Guys like Paulie spent five hundred to a thousand bucks a week. Scotch cost thirty dollars a pint. The hacks used to bring it inside the walls in their lunch pails. We never ran out of booze, because we had six hacks bringing it in six days a week. Depending on what you wanted and how much you were willing to spend, life could be almost bearable."

Wiseguy was reviewed favorably: The *Washington Post* called it an "'amply detailed and entirely fascinating book that amounts to a piece of revisionist history,'" while *New York Daily News* columnist Jimmy Breslin named it "'the best book on crime in America ever written.'" The book was also a commercial success: Within 19 months of its publication, more than a million copies were in print. A few years later, the book was converted into a film called *Goodfellas*, which won a host of awards as the best film of 1990.

From Henry Hill's perspective, however, the publicity generated by the book's success proved less desirable. The Crime Victims Board learned of *Wiseguy* in January 1986, soon after it was published.

On January 31, the Board notified Simon & Schuster: "It has come to our attention that you may have contracted with a person accused or convicted of a crime for the payment of monies to such person." The Board ordered Simon & Schuster to furnish copies of any contracts it had entered into with Hill, to provide the dollar amounts and dates of all payments it had made to Hill, and to suspend all payments to Hill in the future. Simon & Schuster complied with this order. By that time, Simon & Schuster had paid Hill's literary agent $96,250 in advances and royalties on Hill's behalf, and was holding $27,958 for eventual payment to Hill.

The Board reviewed the book and the contract, and on May 21, 1987, issued a Proposed Determination and Order. The Board determined that *Wiseguy* was covered by Section 632-a of the Executive Law, that Simon & Schuster had violated the law by failing to turn over its contract with Hill to the Board and by making payments to Hill, and that all money owed to Hill under the contract had to be turned over to the Board to be held in escrow for the victims of Hill's crimes. The Board ordered Hill to turn over the payments he had already received, and ordered Simon & Schuster to turn over all money payable to Hill at the time or in the future.

Simon & Schuster brought suit in August 1987, . . . seeking a declaration that the *Son of Sam* law violates the First Amendment and an injunction [court order stopping an action] barring the statute's enforcement. . . . [T]he District Court found the statute consistent with the First Amendment. A divided Court of Appeals affirmed [upheld].

Because the Federal Government and most of the States have enacted statutes with similar objectives, the issue is significant and likely to recur. We accordingly granted certiorari [agreed to hear the case], and we now reverse.

A statute is presumptively inconsistent with the First Amendment if it imposes a financial burden on speakers because of the content of their speech. As we emphasized in invalidating a content-based magazine tax, "official scrutiny of the content of publications as the basis for imposing a tax is entirely incompatible with the First Amendment's guarantee of freedom of the press."

This is a notion so engrained in our First Amendment jurisprudence [the science of law] that last Term we found it so "obvious" as to not require explanation. It is but one manifestation of a far broader principle: "Regulations which permit the Government to discriminate on the basis of the content of the message cannot be tolerated under the First Amendment." In the context of financial regulation, it bears repeating, as we did in *Leathers,* that the Government's ability to impose content-based burdens on speech raises the specter that the Government may effectively drive certain ideas or viewpoints from the marketplace. The First Amendment presumptively places this sort of discrimination beyond the power of the Government. As we reiterated in *Leathers,* "'The constitutional right of free expression is . . . intended to remove governmental restraints from the arena of public discussion, putting the decision as to what views shall be voiced largely into the hands of each of us . . . in the belief that no other approach would comport with the premise of individual dignity and choice upon which our political system rests.'"

The *Son of Sam* law is such a content-based statute. It singles out income derived from expressive activity for a burden the State places on no other income, and it is directed only at works with a specified content. Whether the First Amendment "speaker" is considered to be Henry Hill, whose income the statute places in escrow because of the story he has told, or Simon & Schuster, which can publish books about crime with the assistance of only those criminals willing to forgo remuneration for at least five years, the statute plainly imposes a financial disincentive only on speech of a particular content.

The Board tries unsuccessfully to distinguish the *Son of Sam* law from the discriminatory tax at issue in *Arkansas Writers' Project*. While the *Son of Sam* law escrows all of the speaker's speech-derived income for at least five years, rather than taxing a percentage of it outright, this difference can hardly serve as the basis for disparate treatment under the First Amendment. Both forms of financial burden operate as disincentives to speak; indeed, in many cases it will be impossible to discern in advance which type of regulation will be more costly to the speaker.

The Board next argues that discriminatory financial treatment is suspect under the First Amendment only when the legislature intends to suppress certain ideas. This assertion is incorrect; our cases have consistently held that "[i]llicit legislative intent is not the *sine qua non* [without which nothing] of a violation of the First Amendment." Simon & Schuster need adduce [offer] "no evidence of an improper censorial motive." As we concluded in *Minneapolis Star*, "[w]e have long recognized that even regulations aimed at proper governmental concerns can restrict unduly the exercise of rights protected by the First Amendment."

Finally, the Board claims that even if the First Amendment prohibits content-based financial regulation specifically of the *media*, the *Son of Sam* law is different, because it imposes a general burden on any "entity" contracting with a convicted person to transmit that person's speech. This argument falters on both semantic and constitutional grounds. Any "entity" that enters into such a contract becomes by definition a medium of communication, if it wasn't one already. In any event, the characterization of an entity as a member of the "media" is irrelevant for these purposes. The Government's power to impose content-based financial disincentives on speech surely does not vary with the identify of the speaker.

The *Son of Sam* law establishes a financial disincentive to create or publish works with a particular content. In order to justify such differential treatment, "the State must show that its regulation is necessary to serve a compelling state interest and is narrowly drawn to achieve that end."

The Board disclaims, as it must, any state interest in suppressing descriptions of crime out of solicitude for the sensibilities of readers. As we have often had occasion to repeat, "'[T]he fact that society may find speech offensive is not a sufficient reason for suppressing it. Indeed, if it is the speaker's opinion that gives offense, that consequence is a reason for according it constitutional protection.'" "'If there is a bedrock principle underlying the First Amendment, it is that the Government may not prohibit the expression of an idea simply because society finds the idea itself offensive or disagreeable.'" The Board thus does not assert any interest in limiting whatever anguish Henry Hill's victims may suffer from reliving their victimization.

There can be little doubt, on the other hand, that the State has a compelling interest in ensuring that victims of crime are compensated by those who harm them. Every State has a body of . . . law serving exactly this interest. The State's interest in preventing wrongdoers from dissipating their assets before victims can recover explains the existence of the State's statutory provisions for prejudgment

remedies and orders of restitution. We have recognized
the importance of this interest before, in the Sixth
Amendment context.

The State likewise has an undisputed compelling interest
in ensuring that criminals do not profit from their crimes.
Like most if not all States, New York has long recognized
the "fundamental equitable principle" that "[n]o one shall
be permitted to profit by his own fraud, or to take advantage of his own wrong, or to found any claim upon his
own iniquity, or to acquire property by his own crime."
The force of this interest is evidenced by the State's statutory provisions for the forfeiture of the proceeds and in-
strumentalities of crime.

The parties debate whether book royalties can properly be
termed the profits of crime, but that is a question we need
not address here. For the purposes of this case, we can assume without deciding that the income escrowed by the
Son of Sam law represents the fruits of crime. We need
only conclude that the State has a compelling interest in
depriving criminals of the profits of their crimes, and in
using these funds to compensate victims.

The Board attempts to define the State's interest more
narrowly, as "ensuring that criminals do not profit from
storytelling about their crimes before their victims have a
meaningful opportunity to be compensated for their injuries." Here the Board is on far shakier ground. The
Board cannot explain why the State should have any
greater interest in compensating victims from the proceeds of such "storytelling" than from any of the criminal's other assets. Nor can the Board offer any justification for a distinction between this expressive activity and
any other activity in connection with its interest in trans-

ferring the fruits of crime from criminals to their victims.
Thus even if the State can be said to have an interest in
classifying a criminal's assets in this manner, that interest
is hardly compelling.

We have rejected similar assertions of a compelling interest in the past. In *Arkansas Writers' Project* and *Minneapolis Star*, we observed that while the State certainly
has an important interest in raising revenue through taxation, that interest hardly justified selective taxation of the
press, as it was completely unrelated to a press/non-press
distinction. Likewise, in *Carey v. Brown*, we recognized
the State's interest in preserving privacy by prohibiting
residential picketing, but refused to permit the State to
ban only nonlabor picketing. This was because "nothing
in the content-based labor-nonlabor distinction has any
bearing whatsoever on privacy." Much the same is true
here. The distinction drawn by the *Son of Sam* law has
nothing to do with the State's interest in transferring the
proceeds of crime from criminals to their victims.

Like the government entities in the above cases, the Board
has taken the *effect* of the statute and posited that effect
as the State's interest. If accepted, this sort of circular defense can sidestep judicial review of almost any statute,
because it makes all statutes look narrowly tailored. As
Judge Newman pointed out in his dissent from the opinion of the Court of Appeals, such an argument "eliminates
the entire inquiry concerning the validity of content-
based discriminations. Every content-based discrimination
could be upheld by simply observing that the state is anx-
ious to regulate the designated category of speech."

In short, the State has a compelling interest in compensating victims from the fruits of the crime, but little if any

interest in limiting such compensation to the proceeds of the wrongdoer's speech about the crime. We must therefore determine whether the *Son of Sam* law is narrowly tailored to advance the former, not the latter, objective.

As a means of ensuring that victims are compensated from the proceeds of crime, the *Son of Sam* law is significantly overinclusive. As counsel for the Board conceded . . . , the statute applies to works on *any* subject, provided that they express the author's thoughts or recollections about his crime, however tangentially or incidentally. In addition, the statute's broad definition of "person convicted of a crime" enables the Board to escrow the income of any author who admits in his work to having committed a crime, whether or not the author was ever actually accused or convicted.

These two provisions combine to encompass a potentially very large number of works. Had the *Son of Sam* law been in effect at the time and place of publication, it would have escrowed payment for such works as *The Autobiography of Malcolm X*, which describes crimes committed by the civil rights leader before he became a public figure; *Civil Disobedience*, in which Thoreau acknowledges his refusal to pay taxes and recalls his experience in jail; and even the *Confessions of Saint Augustine*, in which the author laments "my past foulness and the carnal corruptions of my soul," one instance of which involved the theft of pears from a neighboring vineyard. *Amicus* [friend of the court] Association of American Publishers, Inc., has submitted a sobering bibliography listing hundreds of works by American prisoners and ex-prisoners, many of which contain descriptions of the crimes for which the authors were incarcerated, including works by such authors as Emma Goldman and Martin Luther King,

Jr. A list of prominent figures whose autobiographies would be subject to the statute if written is not difficult to construct: The list could include Sir Walter Raleigh, who was convicted of treason after a dubiously conducted 1603 trial; Jesse Jackson, who was arrested in 1963 for trespass and resisting arrest after attempting to be served at a lunch counter in North Carolina; and Bertrand Russell, who was jailed for seven days at the age of 89 for participating in a sit-down protest against nuclear weapons. The argument that a statute like the *Son of Sam* law would prevent publication of *all* of these works is hyperbole - some would have been written without compensation - but the *Son of Sam* law clearly reaches a wide range of literature that does not enable a criminal to profit from his crime while a victim remains uncompensated.

Should a prominent figure write his autobiography at the end of his career, and include in an early chapter a brief recollection of having stolen (in New York) a nearly worthless item as a youthful prank, the Board would control his entire income from the book for five years, and would make that income available to all of the author's creditors, despite the fact that the statute of limitations for this minor incident had long since run. That the *Son of Sam* law can produce such an outcome indicates that the statute is, to say the least, not narrowly tailored to achieve the State's objective of compensating crime victims from the profits of crime.

The Federal Government and many of the States have enacted statutes designed to serve purposes similar to that served by the *Son of Sam* law. Some of these statutes may be quite different from New York's, and we have no occasion to determine the constitutionality of these other laws. We conclude simply that in the *Son of Sam* law, New

York has singled out speech on a particular subject for a financial burden that it places on no other speech and no other income. The State's interest in compensating victims from the fruits of crime is a compelling one, but the *Son of Sam* law is not narrowly tailored to advance that objective. As a result, the statute is inconsistent with the First Amendment.

The judgment of the Court of Appeals is accordingly reversed.

THE U.S. CONSTITUTION

PREAMBLE

We the people of the United States, in order to form a more perfect union, establish justice, insure domestic tranquility, provide for the common defense, promote the general welfare, and secure the blessings of liberty to ourselves and our posterity, do ordain and establish this Constitution for the United States of America.

ARTICLE I

Section 1. All legislative powers herein granted shall be vested in a Congress of the United States, which shall consist of a Senate and House of Representatives.

Section 2. (1) The House of Representatives shall be composed of members chosen every second year by the people of several states, and the electors in each state shall have the qualifications requisite for electors of the most numerous branch of the State Legislature.

(2) No person shall be a Representative who shall not have attained to the age of twenty-five years, and been seven years a citizen of the United States, and who shall not, when elected, be an inhabitant of that state in which he shall be chosen.

(3) Representatives and direct taxes shall be apportioned among the several states which may be included within this union, according to their respective numbers, which shall be determined by adding to the whole number of free persons, including those bound to service for a term of years, and excluding Indians not taxed, three-fifths of all other persons. The actual enumeration shall be made

within three years after the first meeting of the Congress
of the United States, and within every subsequent term of
ten years, in such manner as they shall be law direct. The
number of Representatives shall not exceed one for every
thirty thousand, but each state shall have at least one Representative; and until such enumeration shall be made, the
State of New Hampshire shall be entitled to choose three,
Massachusetts eight, Rhode Island and Providence Planta-
tions one, Connecticut five, New York six, New Jersey
four, Pennsylvania eight, Delaware one, Maryland six, Vir-
ginia ten, North Carolina five, South Carolina five, and
Georgia three.

(4) When vacancies happen in the representation from
any state, the executive authority thereof shall issue Writs
of Election to fill such vacancies.

(5) The House of Representatives shall choose their
Speaker and other Officers; and shall have the sole power
of impeachment.

Section 3. (1) The Senate of the United States shall be
composed of two Senators from each state, chosen by the
legislature thereof, for six years; and each Senator shall
have one vote.

(2) Immediately after they shall be assembled in consequence of the first election, they shall be divided as equally as may be into three classes. The seats of the Senators
of the first class shall be vacated at the expiration of the
second year, of the second class at the expiration of the
fourth year, and of the third class at the expiration of the
sixth year, so that one-third may be chosen every second
year; and if vacancies happen by resignation, or otherwise,
during the recess of the legislature of any state, the execu-

tive thereof may take temporary appointments until the next meeting of the legislature, which shall then fill such vacancies.

(3) No person shall be a Senator who shall not have attained to the age of thirty years, and been nine years a citizen of the United States, and who shall not, when elected, be an inhabitant of that state for which he shall be chosen.

(4) The Vice President of the United States shall be President of the Senate, but shall have no vote, unless they be equally divided.

(5) The Senate shall choose their other Officers, and also a President pro tempore, in the absence of the Vice President, or when he shall exercise the Office of President of the United States.

(6) The Senate shall have the sole power to try all impeachments. When sitting for that purpose, they shall be on oath or affirmation. When the President of the United States is tried, the Chief Justice shall preside: and no person shall be convicted without the concurrence of two-thirds of the members present.

(7) Judgment in cases of impeachment shall not extend further than to removal from office, and disqualification to hold and enjoy any office of honor, trust, or profit under the United States: but the party convicted shall nevertheless be liable and subject to indictment, trial, judgment, and punishment, according to law.

Section 4. (1) The times, places and manner of holding elections for Senators and Representatives, shall be pre-

scribed in each state by the legislature thereof; but the
Congress may at any time by law make or alter such regulations, except as to the places of choosing Senators.

(2) The Congress shall assemble at least once in every
year, and such meeting shall be on the first Monday in
December, unless they shall by law appoint a different
day.

Section 5. (1) Each House shall be the judge of the elections, returns, and qualifications of its own members, and
a majority of each shall constitute a quorum to do business; but a smaller number may adjourn from day to day,
and may be authorized to compel the attendance of absent
members, in such manner, and under such penalties as
each House may provide.

(2) Each House may determine the rules of its proceedings, punish its members for disorderly behavior, and,
with the concurrence of two-thirds, expel a member.

(3) Each House shall keep a journal of its proceedings,
and from time to time publish the same, excepting such
parts as may in their judgment require secrecy; and the
yeas and nays of the members of either House on any
question shall, at the desire of one-fifth of those present,
be entered on the journal.

(4) Neither House, during the Session of Congress, shall,
without the consent of the other, adjourn for more than
three days, nor to any other place than that in which the
two Houses shall be sitting.

Section 6. (1) The Senators and Representatives shall receive a compensation for their services, to be ascertained

by law, and paid out of the Treasury of the United States. They shall in all cases, except treason, felony and breach of the peace, be privileged from arrest during their attendance at the session of their respective Houses, and in going to and returning from the same; and for any speech or debate in either House, they shall not be questioned in any other place.

(2) No Senator or Representative shall, during the time for which he was elected, be appointed to any civil office under the authority of the United States, which shall have been created, or the emoluments whereof shall have been increased during such time and no person holding any office under the United States, shall be a member of either House during his continuance in office.

Section 7. (1) All bills for raising revenue shall originate in the House of Representatives; but the Senate may propose or concur with amendments as on other bills.

(2) Every bill which shall have passed the House of Representatives and the Senate, shall, before it become a law, be presented to the President of the United States; if he approve he shall sign it, but if not he shall return it, with his objections to the House in which it shall have originated, who shall enter the objections at large on their journal, and proceed to reconsider it. If after such reconsideration two-thirds of that House shall agree to pass the bill, it shall be sent together with the objections, to the other House, by which it shall likewise be reconsidered, and if approved by two-thirds of that House, it shall become a law. But in all such cases the votes of both Houses shall be determined by yeas and nays, and the names of the persons voting for and against the bill shall be entered on the journal of each House respectively. If any bill shall not

be returned by the President within ten days (Sundays excepted) after it shall have been presented to him, the same shall be a law, in like manner as if he had signed it, unless the Congress by their adjournment prevent its return in which case it shall not be a law.

(3) Every order, resolution, of vote, to which the concurrence of the Senate and House of Representatives may be necessary (except on a question of adjournment) shall be presented to the President of the United States; and before the same shall take effect, shall be approved by him, or being disapproved by him, shall be repassed by two-thirds of the Senate and House of Representatives, according to the rules and limitations prescribed in the case of a bill.

Section 8. (1) The Congress shall have the power to lay and collect taxes, duties, imposts and excises, to pay the debts and provide for the common defense and general welfare of the United States; but all duties, imposts and excises shall be uniform throughout the United States;

(2) To borrow money on the credit of the United States;

(3) To regulate commerce with foreign nations, and among the several states, and with the Indian Tribes;

(4) To establish an uniform Rule of Naturalization, and uniform laws on the subject of bankruptcies throughout the United States;

(5) To coin money, regulate the value thereof, and of foreign coin, and fix the standard of weights and measures;

(6) To provide for the punishment of counterfeiting the securities and current coin of the United States;

(7) To establish Post Offices and Post Roads;

(8) To promote the progress of science and useful arts, by securing for limited times to authors and inventors the exclusive right to their respective writings and discoveries;

(9) To constitute tribunals inferior the Supreme Court;

(10) To define and punish piracies and felonies committed on the high seas, and offenses against the Law of Nations;

(11) To declare war, grant Letters of Marque and Reprisal, and make rules concerning captures on land and water;

(12) To raise and support armies, but no appropriation of money to that use shall be for a longer term than two years;

(13) To provide and maintain a Navy;

(14) To make rules for the government and regulation of the land and naval forces;

(15) To provide for calling forth the Militia to execute the laws of the Union, suppress insurrections and repel invasions;

(16) To provide for organizing, arming, and disciplining, the Militia, and for governing such part of them as may be employed in the service of the United States, reserving to the states respectively, the appointment of the Officers,

and the authority of training the Militia according to the discipline prescribed by Congress;

(17) To exercise exclusive legislation in all cases whatsoever, over such district (not exceeding ten miles square) as may, be cession of particular states, and the acceptance of Congress, become the Seat of the Government of the United States, and to exercise like authority over all places purchased by the consent of the legislature of the state in which the same shall be, for the erection of forts, magazines, arsenals, dockyards, and other needful buildings; -- and

(18) To make all laws which shall be necessary and proper for carrying into execution the foregoing powers, and all other powers vested by this Constitution in the Government of the United States, or in any Department or Officer thereof.

Section 9. (1) The migration or importation of such persons as any of the states now existing shall think proper to admit, shall not be prohibited by the Congress prior to the year one thousand eight hundred and eight, but a tax or duty may be imposed on such importation, not exceeding ten dollars for each person.

(2) The privilege of the Writ of Habeas Corpus shall not be suspended, unless when in cases of rebellion or invasion the public safety may require it.

(3) No Bill of Attainder or ex post facto law shall be passed.

(4) No capitation, or other direct, tax shall be laid, unless in proportion to the Census or enumeration herein before directed to be taken.

(5) No tax or duty shall be laid on articles exported from any state.

(6) No preference shall be given by any regulation of commerce or revenue to th ports of one state over those of another: nor shall vessels bound to, or from, one state be obliged to enter, clear, or pay duties in another.

(7) No money shall be drawn from the Treasury, but in consequence eof appropriations made by law; and a regular statement and account of the receipts and expenditures of all public money shall be published from time to time.

(8) No title of nobility shall be granted by the United States: and no person holding any office of profit or trust under them, shall, without the consent of the Congress, accept of any present, emolument, office, or title, of any kind whatever, from any King, Prince, or foreign State.

Section 10. (1) No state shall enter into any treaty, alliance, or confederation; grant Letter of Marque and Reprisal; coin money; emit bills of credit; make any thing but gold and silver coin a tender in payment of debts; pass and Bill of Attainder, ex post facto law, or law impairing the obligation of contracts, or grant any title of nobility.

(2) No state shall, without the consent of the Congress, lay any imposts or duties on imports or exports, except what may be absolutely necessary for executing its inspection laws: and the net produce of all duties and imposts, laid by any state on imports or exports, shall be for the use of

the Treasury of the United States; and all such laws shall be subject to the revision and control of the Congress.

(3) No state shall, without the consent of Congress, lay any duty of tonnage, keep troops, or ships of war in time of peace, enter into any agreement or compact with another state, or with a foreign power, or engage in war, unless actually invaded, or in such imminent danger as will not admit of delay.

ARTICLE II

Section 1. (1) The executive power shall be vested in a President of the United States of America. He shall hold his office during the term of four years, and, together with the Vice President, chosen for the same term, be elected, as follows:

(2) Each state shall appoint, in such manner as the legislature thereof may direct, a number of electors, equal to the whole number os Senators and Representatives to which the state may be entitled in the Congress; but no Senator or Representative, or person holding an office of trust or profit under the United States, shall be appointed an Elector.

(3) The Electors shall meet in their respective states, and vote by ballot for two persons, of whom one at least shall not be an inhabitant of the same state with themselves. And they shall make a list of all the persons voted for, and of the number of votes for each; which list they shall sign and certify, and transmit sealed to the Seat of the Government of the United States, directed to the President of the Senate. The President of the Senate shall, in the presence of the Senate and House of Representatives,

open all the certificates, and the votes shall then be counted. The person having the greatest number of votes shall be the President, if such number be a majority of the whole number of Electors appointed; and if there be more than one who have such majority, and have an equal number of votes, then the House of Representatives shall immediately choose by ballot one of them for President; and if no person have a majority, then from the five highest on the list the said House shall in like manner choose the President. But in choosing the President, the votes shall be taken by states the representation from each state having one vote; a quorum for this purpose shall consist of a member or members from two-thirds of the states, and a majority of all the states shall be necessary to a choice. In every case, after the choice of the President, the person having the greater number of votes of the Electors shall be the Vice President. But if there should remain two or more who have equal votes, the Senate shall choose from them by ballot the Vice President.

(4) The Congress may determine the time of choosing the Electors, and the day on which they shall give their votes; which day shall be the same throughout the United States.

(5) No person except a natural born citizen, or a citizen of the United States, at the time of the adoption of this Constitution, shall be eligible to the Office of President; neither shall any person be eligible to that Office who shall not have attained to the age of thirty-five years, and been fourteen years a resident within the United States.

(6) In case of the removal of the President from Office, or of his death, resignation or inability to discharge the powers and duties of the said Office, the same shall devolve on the Vice President, and the Congress may by law

provide for the case of removal, death, resignation of inability, both of the President and Vice President, declaring
what Officer shall then act as President, and such Officer
shall act accordingly, until the disability be removed, or a
President shall be elected.

(7) The President shall, at stated times, receive for his
services, a compensation, which shall neither be increased
nor diminished during the period for which he shall have
been elected, and he shall not receive within that period
any other emolument from the United States, or any of
them.

(8) Before he enter on the execution of his Office, he
shall take the following Oath or Affirmation: "I do sol-
emnly swear (or affirm) that I will faithfully execute the
Office of President of the United States, and will to the
best of my ability, preserve, protect and defend the Constitution of the United States."

Section 2. (1) The President shall be Commander in Chief
of the Army and Navy of the United States, and of the
militia of the several states, when called into the actual
service of the United States; he may require the opinion,
in writing, of the principal Officer in each of the Executive Departments, upon any subject relating to the duties
of their respective Offices, and he shall have power to
grant reprieves and pardons for offenses against the United States, except in cases of impeachment.

(2) He shall have power, by and with the advice and consent of the Senate to make treaties, provided two-thirds of
the Senators present concur; and he shall nominate, and
by and with the advice and consent of the Senate, shall appoint Ambassadors, other public Ministers and Consuls,

Judges of the supreme Court, and all other Officers of the United States, whose appointments are not herein otherwise provided for, and which shall be established by law; but the Congress may be law vest the appointment of such inferior Officers, as they think proper, in the President alone, in the courts of law, or in the Heads of Departments.

(3) The President shall have power to fill up all vacancies that may happen during the recess of the Senate, by granting commissions which shall expire at the end of their next Session.

Section 3. He shall from time to time give to the Congress information of the State of the Union, and recommend to their consideration such measures as he shall judge necessary and expedient; he may, on extraordinary occasions, convene both Houses, or either of them, and in case of disagreement between them, with respect to the time of adjournment, he may adjourn them to such time as he shall think proper; he shall receive Ambassadors and other public Ministers; he shall take care that the laws be faithfully executed, and shall commission all the Officers of the United States.

Section 4. The President, Vice President and all civil Officers of the United States, shall be removed from office on impeachment for, and conviction of, treason, bribery, or other high crimes and misdemeanors.

ARTICLE III

Section 1. The judicial power of the United States, shall be vested in one supreme Court, and in such inferior courts as the Congress may from time to time ordain and establish. The Judges, both of the supreme and inferior courts, shall hold their Offices during good behaviour, and shall, at stated times, receive for their services a compensation, which shall not be diminished during their continuance in office.

Section 2. (1) The judicial power shall extend to all cases, in law and equity, arising under this Constitution, the laws of the United States, and treaties made, or which shall be made, under their authority; -- to all cases affecting Ambassadors, other public Ministers and Consuls; -- to all cases of admiralty and maritime jurisdiction; -- to controversies to which the United States shall be a party; -- to controversies between two or more states; -- between a state and citizens of another state; -- between citizens of different states; -- between citizens of the same state claiming lands under the grants of different states, and between a state, or the citizens thereof, and foreign states, citizens or subjects.

(2) In all cases affecting Ambassadors, other public Ministers and Consuls, and those in which a state shall be a party, the supreme Court shall have original jurisdiction. In all the other cases before mentioned, the supreme Court shall have appellate jurisdiction, both as to law and fact, with such exceptions, and under such regulations as the Congress shall make.

(3) The trial of all crimes, except in cases of impeachment, shall be by jury; and such trial shall be held in the state where the said crimes shall have been committed; but when not committed within any state, the trial shall be at such place or places as the Congress may be law have directed.

Section 3. (1) Treason against the United States, shall consist only in levying war against them, or, in adhering to their enemies, giving them aid and comfort. No person shall be convicted of treason unless on the testimony of two witnesses to the same overt act, or on confession in open Court.

(2) The Congress shall have power to declare the punishment of treason, but no Attainder of Treason shall work corruption of blood, or forfeiture except during the life of the person attainted.

ARTICLE IV

Section 1. Full faith and credit shall be given in each state to the public acts, records, and judicial proceedings of every other state. And the Congress may by general laws prescribe the manner in which such acts, records and proceedings shall be proved, and the effect thereof.

Section 2. (1) The citizens of each state shall be entitled to all privileges and immunities of citizens in the several states.

(2) A person charged in any state with treason, felony, or other crime, who shall flee from justice, and be found in another state, shall on demand of the executive authority of the state from which he fled, be delivered up, to be removed to the state having jurisdiction of the crime.

(3) No person held to service or labour in one state, under the laws thereof, escaping into another, shall, in consequence of any law or regulation therein, be discharged from such service or labour, but shall be delivered up on

claim of the party to whom such service or labour may be due.

Section 3. (1) New states may be admitted by the Congress into this Union; but no new state shall be formed or erected within the jurisdiction of any other state; nor any state be formed by the junction of two or more states, or parts of states, without the consent of the legislatures of the states concerned as well as of the Congress.

(2) The Congress shall have power to dispose of and make all needful rules and regulations respecting the territory or other property belonging to the United States; and nothing in this Constitution shall be so construed as to prejudice any claims of the United States, or of any particular state.

Section 4. The United States shall guarantee to every state in this Union a Republican form of government, and shall protect each of them against invasion; and on application of the Legislature, or of the Executive (when the Legislature cannot be convened) against domestic violence.

ARTICLE V

The Congress, whenever two-thirds of both Houses shall deem it necessary, shall propose amendments to this Constitution, or, on the application of the Legislatures of two-thirds of the several states, shall call a convention for proposing amendments, which, in either case, shall be valid to all intents and purposes, as part of this constitution, when ratified by the Legislatures of three-fourths of the several states, or by conventions in three-fourths thereof, as the one or the other mode of ratification may be proposed by the Congress; provided that no amendment which may be made prior to the year one thousand eight hundred and eight shall in any manner affect the first and fourth clauses in the Ninth Section of the first Article; and that no state, without its consent, shall be deprived of its equal suffrage in the Senate.

ARTICLE VI

(1) All debts contracted and engagements entered into, before the adoption of this Constitution shall be as valid against the United States under this Constitution, as under the Confederation.

(2) This Constitution, and the laws of the United States which shall be made in pursuance thereof; and all treaties made, or which shall be made, under the authority of the United States, shall be the supreme law of the land; and the Judges in every state shall be bound thereby, any thing in the Constitution or laws of any state to the contrary notwithstanding.

(3) The Senators and Representatives before mentioned, and the Members of the several State Legislatures, and all executive and judicial Officers, both of the United States and of the several states, shall be bound by oath or affirmation, to support this Constitution; but no religious test shall ever be required as a qualification to any Office or public trust under the United States.

ARTICLE VII

The ratification of the Conventions of nine states shall be sufficient for the establishment of this Constitution between the states so ratifying the same.

AMENDMENT I (1791)

Congress shall make no law respecting an establishment of religion, or prohibiting the free exercise thereof; or abridging the freedom of speech, or of the press; or the right of the people peaceably to assemble, and to petition the Government for a redress of grievances.

AMENDMENT II (1791)

A well regulated Militia, being necessary to the security of a free State, the right of the people to keep and bear arms, shall not be infringed.

AMENDMENT III (1791)

No soldier shall, in time of peace be quartered in any house, without the consent of the owner, nor in time of war, but in a manner to be prescribed by law.

AMENDMENT IV (1791)

The right of the people to be secure in their persons, houses, papers, and effects, against unreasonable searches and seizures, shall not be violated, and no warrants shall issue, but upon probable cause, supported by oath or affirmation, and particularly describing the place to be searched, and the persons or things to be seized.

AMENDMENT V (1791)

No person shall be held to answer for a capital, or otherwise infamous crime, unless on a presentment or indictment of a Grand Jury, except in cases arising in the land or naval forces, or in the Militia, when in actual service in time of war or public danger; nor shall any person be subject for the same offense to be twice put in jeopardy of life or limb; nor shall be compelled in any criminal case to be a witness against himself, nor be deprived of life, liberty, or property, without due process of law; nor shall private property be taken for public use, without just compensation.

AMENDMENT VI (1791)

In all criminal prosecutions, the accused shall enjoy the right to a speedy and public trial, by an impartial jury of the state and district wherein the crime shall have been committed, which district shall have been previously ascertained by law, and to be informed of the nature and cause of the accusation; to be confronted with the witnesses against him; to have compulsory process for obtaining witnesses in his favor, and to have the assistance of counsel for his defense.

AMENDMENT VII (1791)

In suits at common law, where the value in controversy shall exceed twenty dollars, the right of trial by jury shall be preserved, and no fact tried by jury, shall be otherwise re-examined in any Court of the United States, than according to the rules of the common law.

AMENDMENT VIII (1791)

Excessive bail shall not be required, nor excessive fines imposed, nor cruel and unusual punishments inflicted.

AMENDMENT IX (1791)

The enumeration in the Constitution, of certain rights, shall not be construed to deny or disparage others retained by the people.

AMENDMENT X (1791)

The powers not delegated to the United States by the Constitution, nor prohibited by it to the States, are reserved to the States respectively, or to the people.

AMENDMENT XI (1798)

The judicial power of the United States shall not be construed to extend to any suit in law or equity, commenced or prosecuted against one of the United States by citizens of another state, or by citizens or subjects of any foreign state.

AMENDMENT XII (1804)

The Electors shall meet in their respective states and vote by ballot for President and Vice-President, one of whom, at least, shall not be an inhabitant of the same stat with themselves; they shall name in their ballots the person voted for as President, and in distinct ballots the person voted for as Vice-President, and they shall make distinct lists of all persons voted for as President, and of all persons voted for as Vice-President, and of the number of votes for each, which lists they shall sign and certify, and transmit sealed to the seat of the government of the United States, directed to the President of the Senate; -- the President of the Senate shall, in the presence of the Senate and House of Representatives, open all the certificates and the votes shall then be counted; -- the person having the greatest number of votes for President, shall be the President, if such number be a majority of the persons having the highest numbers not exceeding three on the list of those voted for as President, the House of Representatives shall choose immediately, by ballot, the President. But in choosing the President, the votes shall be taken by states, the representation from each state having one vote; a quorum for his purpose shall consist of a member or members from two-thirds of the states, and a majority of all the states shall be necessary to a choice. And if the House of Representatives shall not choose a President whenever the right of choice shall devolve upon them before the fourth day of March next following, then the Vice-President shall act as President, as in the case of the death or other constitutional disability of the President. -- The person having the greatest number of votes as Vice-President, shall be the Vice-President, if such number be a majority of the whole number of Electors appointed, and if no person have a majority, then from the two highest numbers on the list, the Senate shall choose the Vice-President; a quorum for the purpose shall consist of two-thirds of the whole number of Senators, and a majority of the whole number shall be necessary to a choice. But no person constitutionally ineligible to the office of President shall be eligible to that of Vice-President of the United States.

AMENDMENT XIII (1865)

Section 1. Neither slavery nor involuntary servitude, except as a punishment for crime whereof the party shall have been duly convicted, shall exist within the United States, or any place subject to their jurisdiction.

Section 2. Congress shall have power to enforce this article by appropriate legislation.

AMENDMENT XIV (1868)

Section 1. All persons born or naturalized in the United States, and subject to the jurisdiction thereof, are citizens of the United States and of the state wherein they reside. No state shall make or enforce any law which shall abridge the privileges or immunities of citizens of the United States; nor shall any state deprive any person of life, liberty, or property, without due process of law; nor deny to any person within its jurisdiction the equal protection of the laws.

Section 2. Representatives shall be apportioned among the several states according to their respective numbers, counting the whole number of persons in each State excluding Indians not taxed. But when the right to vote at any election for the choice of electors for President and Vice President of the United States, Representatives in Congress, the Executive and Judicial officers of a state, or the members of the Legislature thereof, is denied to any of the male inhabitants of such state, being twenty-one years of age, and citizens of the United States, or in any way abridged, except for participation in rebellion, or other crime, the basis of representation therein shall be reduced in the proportion which the number of such male citizens shall bear to the whole number of male citizens twenty-one years of age in such state.

Section 3. No person shall be a Senator or Representative in Congress, or elector of President and Vice President, or hold any office, civil or military, under the United States, or under any state, who having previously taken an oath, as a member of Congress, or as an officer of the United States, or as a member of any state legislature, or as an executive or judicial officer of any state, to support the Constitution of the United States, shall have engaged in insurrection or rebellion against the same, or given aid or comfort to the enemies thereof. But Congress may by a vote of two-thirds of each House, remove such disability.

Section 4. The validity of the public debt of the United States, authorized by law, including debts incurred for payment of pensions and bounties for services in suppressing insurrection or rebellion, shall not be questioned. But neither the United States nor any state shall assume or pay any debt or obligation incurred in aid of insurrection or rebellion against the United States, or any claim for the loss or emancipation of any slave; but all such debts, obligations and claims shall be held illegal and void.

Section 5. The Congress shall have power to enforce, by appropriate legislation, the provisions of this article.

AMENDMENT XV (1870)

Section 1. The right of citizens of the United States to vote shall not be denied or abridged by the United States or by any state on account of race, color, or previous condition of servitude.

Section 2. The Congress shall have power to enforce this article by appropriate legislation.

AMENDMENT XVI (1913)

The Congress shall have power to lay and collect taxes on income, from whatever source derived, without apportionment among the several states, and without regard to any census or enumeration.

AMENDMENT XVII (1913)

(1) The Senate of the United States shall be composed of two Senators from each state, elected by the people thereof, for six years; and each Senator shall have one vote. The electors in each State shall have the qualifications requisite for electors of the most numerous branch of the state legislatures.

(2) When vacancies happen in the representation of any state in the Senate, the executive authority of such state shall issue writs of election to fill such vacancies: *provided,* that the legislature of any state may empower the executive thereof to make temporary appointments until the people fill the vacancies by election as the legislature may direct.

(3) This amendment shall not be so construed as to affect the election or term of any Senator chosen before it becomes valid as part of the Constitution.

AMENDMENT XVIII (1919)

Section 1. After one year from the ratification of this article the manufacture, sale, or transportation of intoxicating liquors within, the importation thereof into, or the exportation thereof from the United States and all territory subject to the jurisdiction thereof for beverage purposes is hereby prohibited.

Section 2. The Congress and the several states shall have concurrent power to enforce this article by appropriate legislation.

Section 3. This article shall be inoperative unless it shall have been ratified as an amendment to the Constitution by the legislatures of the several states, as provided in the Constitution, within seven years from the date of the submission hereof to the states by the Congress.

AMENDMENT XIX (1920)

(1) The right of citizens of the United States to vote shall not be denied or abridged by the United States or by any state on account of sex.

(2) Congress shall have power to enforce this article by appropriate legislation.

AMENDMENT XX (1933)

Section 1. The terms of the President and Vice President shall end at noon on the 20th day of January, and the terms of Senators and Representatives at noon on the 3d day of January, of the years in which such terms would have ended if this article had not been ratified; and the terms of their successors shall then begin.

Section 2. The Congress shall assemble at least once in every year, and such meeting shall begin at noon on the 3d day of January, unless they shall by law appoint a different day.

Section 3. If, at the time fixed for the beginning of the term of the President, the President elect shall have died,

the Vice President elect shall become President. If the
President shall not have been chosen before the time fixed for the beginning of his term, or if the President elect
shall have failed to qualify, then the Vice President elect
shall act as President until a President shall have qualified; and the Congress may by law provide for the case
wherein neither a President elect nor a Vice President
elect shall have qualified, declaring who shall then act as
President, or the manner in which one who is to act shall
be selected, and such person shall act accordingly until a
President or Vice President shall have qualified.

Section 4. The Congress may by law provide for the case
of the death of any of the persons from whom the House
of Representatives may choose a President whenever the
right of choice shall have devolved upon them, and for
the case of the death of any of the persons from whom
the Senate may choose a Vice President whenever the
right of choice shall have devolved upon them.

Section 5. Sections 1 and 2 shall take effect on the 15th
day of October following the ratification of this article.

Section 6. This article shall be inoperative unless it shall
have been ratified as an amendment to the Constitution
by the legislatures of three-fourths of the several states
within seven years from the date of its submission.

AMENDMENT XXI (1933)

Section 1. The eighteenth article of amendment to the
Constitution of the United States is hereby repealed.

Section 2. The transportation or importation into any
state, territory, or possession of the United States for de-

livery or use therein of intoxicating liquors, in violation of the laws thereof, is hereby prohibited.

Section 3. This article shall be inoperative unless it shall have been ratified as an amendment to the Constitution by conventions in the several states, as provided in the Constitution, within seven years from the date of the submission hereof to the states by the Congress.

AMENDMENT XXII (1951)

Section 1. No person shall be elected to the office of the President more than twice, and no person who has held the office of President, or acted as President, for more than two ears of a term to which some other person was elected President shall be elected to the office of President more than once. But this Article shall not apply to any person holding the office of President when this Article was proposed by the Congress, and shall not prevent any person who may be holding the office of President, or acting as President, during the term within which this Article becomes operative from holding the office of President or acting as President during the remainder of such term.

Section 2. This article shall be inoperative unless it shall have been ratified as an amendment to the Constitution by the legislatures of three-fourths of the several states within seven years from the date of its submission to the states by the Congress.

AMENDMENT XXIII (1961)

Section 1. The District constituting the seat of Government of the United States shall appoint in such manner as the Congress may direct:

A number of electors of President and Vice President equal to the whole number of Senators and Representatives in Congress to which the District would be entitled if it were a state, but in no event more than the least populous state; they shall be in addition to those appointed by the states, but they shall be considered, for the purposes of the election of President and Vice President, to be electors appointed by a state; and they shall meet in the District and perform such duties as provided by the twelfth article of amendment.

Section 2. The Congress shall have power to enforce this article by appropriate legislation.

AMENDMENT XXIV (1964)

Section 1. The right of citizens of the United States to vote in any primary or other election for President or Vice President, for electors for President or Vice President, or for Senator or Representative in Congress, shall not be denied or abridged by the United States, or any state by reason of failure to pay any poll tax or other tax.

Section 2. The Congress shall have power to enforce this article by appropriate legislation.

AMENDMENT XXV (1967)

Section 1. In case of the removal of the President from office or of his death or resignation, the Vice President shall become President.

Section 2. Whenever there is a vacancy in the office of the Vice President, the President shall nominate a Vice President who shall take office upon confirmation by a majority vote of both Houses of Congress.

Section 3. Whenever the President transmits to the President pro tempore of the Senate and the Speaker of the House of Representatives his written declaration that he is unable to discharge the powers and duties of his office, and until he transmits to them a written declaration to the contrary, such powers and duties shall be discharged by the Vice President as Acting President.

Section 4. Whenever the Vice President and a majority of either the principal officers of the executive departments or of such other body as Congress may by law provide, transmit to the President pro tempore of the Senate and the Speaker of the House of Representatives their written declaration that the President is unable to discharge the powers and duties of his office, the Vice President shall immediately assume the powers and duties of the office as Acting President.

Thereafter, when the President transmits to the President pro tempore of the Senate and the Speaker of the House of Representatives his written declaration that no inability exists, he shall resume the powers and duties of his office unless the Vice President and a majority of either the principal officers of the executive department or of such other body as Congress may by law provide, transmit within four days to the President pro tempore of the Senate and the Speaker of the House of Representatives their written declaration and the President is unable to discharge the powers and duties of his office. Thereupon Congress shall decide the issue, assembling within forty-eight hours for that purpose if not in session. If the Congress, within twenty-one days after receipt of the latter written declaration, or, if Congress is not in session, within twenty-one days after Congress is required to assemble, determines by two-thirds vote of both Houses that the President is unable to discharge the power and duties of his office, the Vice President shall continue to discharge the same as Acting President; otherwise, the President shall resume the powers and duties of his office.

AMENDMENT XXVI (1971)

Section 1. The right of citizens of the United States, who are eighteen years of age or older, to vote shall not be denied or abridged by the United States or by any state on account of age.

Section 2. The Congress shall have power to enforce this article by appropriate legislation.

AMENDMENT XXVII (1992)

No law, varying the compensation for the services of the Senators and Representatives, shall take effect, until an election of Representatives shall have intervened.

BIBLIOGRAPHY

THE SLAVE SHIP CASES

Adams, John Quincy. *Argument of John Quincy Adams Before the Supreme Court of the United States, in the Case of United States v. Cinque.* New York, NY: Negro University Press, 1969.

The Amistad Case: The Most Celebrated Slave Mutiny of the Nineteenth Century. New York, NY: Johnson Reprint Corp., 1968.

Barber, John W. *A History of The Amistad Captives.* New York, NY: Arno Press, 1969.

Cable, Mary. *Black Odyssey: The Case of the Slave Ship Amistad.* New York, NY: Viking Press, 1971.

Hoyt, Edwin P. *The Amistad Affair.* New York, NY: Abelard-Schuman, 1970.

Jones, Howard. *Mutiny on the Amistad.* New York, NY: Oxford University Press, 1987.

Noonan, John Thomas. *The Antelope: The Ordeal of the Recaptured Africans in the Administration of James Monroe and John Quincy Adams.* Berkeley, CA: University of California Press, 1977.

RELIGIOUS LIBERTY

Konvitz, Milton R. *Fundamental Liberties of a Free People: Religion, Speech, Press, Assembly.* Ithaca, NY: Cornell University Press, 1957.

Leahy, James E. *The First Amendment, 1791-1991: Two Hundred Years of Freedom.* Jefferson, NC: McFarland & Co., 1991.

Richards, David A.J. *Toleration and the Constitution.* New York, NY: Oxford University Press, 1986.

Wagman, Robert J. *The First Amendment Book.* New York, NY: World Almanac, 1991.

TREASON

Hurst, James W. *The Law of Treason in the United States: Collected Essays.* Westport, CT: Greenwood Publishing Co., 1971.

Rachlis, Eugene. *They Came to Kill.* New York, NY: Random House, 1961.

West, Rebecca. *The Meaning of Treason.* New York, NY: Viking Press, 1947.

MILITARY JUSTICE

DiMona, Joseph. *Great Court-Martial Cases.* New York, NY: Grossett & Dunlap, 1972.

Sherrill, Robert. *Military Justice is to Justice as Military Music is to Music.* New York, NY: Harper & Row, 1970.

MARIJUANA

Abel, Ernest L. *Marihuana: The First 12,000 Years.* New York, NY: Plenum Press, 1980.

Horowitz, Michael. *An Annotated Bibliography of Timothy Leary.* Hamden, CT: Archon Books, 1988.

Leary, Timothy F. *Changing My Mind, Among Others: Lifetime Writings.* Englewood Cliffs, NJ: Prentice-Hall, 1982.

Merlin, Mark D. *Man and Marijuana: Some Aspects of Their Ancient Relationship.* Rutherford, NJ: Fairleigh Dickinson University Press, 1972.

BIRTH CONTROL

Dienes, C. Thomas. *Law, Politics, and Birth Control.* Urbana, IL: University of Illinois Press, 1972.

Gordon, Linda. *Woman's Body, Woman's Right: Birth Control in America.* New York, NY: Penguin Books, 1990.

Reed, James. *From Private Vice to Public Virtue: The Birth Control Movement and American Society Since 1830.* New York, NY: Basic Books, 1978.

Sloan, Irving J. *The Law Governing Abortion, Contraception and Sterilization.* New York, NY: Oceana Publications, 1988.

BASEBALL

Dworkin, James B. *Owners vs. Players: Baseball and Collective Bargaining.* Boston, MA: Auburn House Publishing Co., 1981.

Flood, Curt (with Richard Carter). *The Way It Is.* New York, NY: Trident Press, 1971.

Kuhn, Bowie (with Martin Appel). *Hardball: The Education of a Baseball Commissioner.* New York, NY: Times Books, 1987.

EQUAL PAY FOR EQUAL WORK

Blau, Francine. *Equal Pay in the Office.* Lexington, MA: Lexington Books, 1977.

Dworaczek, Marian. *Equal Pay for Comparable Work: A Bibliography.* Monticello, IL: Vane Bibliographies, 1984.

Equal Pay for Comparable Work. Washington, DC: Women's Legal Defense Fund, 1983.

Hutner, Frances C. *Equal Pay for Comparable Worth.* New York, NY: Praeger, 1986.

CHILD ABUSE

Broadhurst, Diane D., and James S. Knowller. *The Role of Law Enforcement in the Prevention and Treatment of Child Abuse and Neglect.* Washington, DC: National Center on Child Abuse and Neglect, 1979.

Eberle, Paul. *The Politics of Child Abuse.* Secaucus, NJ: L. Stuart, 1986.

Sloan, Irving J. *Child Abuse: Governing Law and Legislation.* New York, NY: Oceana Publications, 1983.

Tower, Cynthia C. *Child Abuse and Neglect.* Washington, DC: NEA Professional Library, 1987.

Wells, Dorothy P. *Child Abuse, An Annotated Bibliography.* Metuchen, NJ: Scarecrow Press, 1980.

THE "SON OF SAM" LAW

Fletcher, George P. *With Justice For Some: Victims' Rights in Criminal Trials.* Reading, MA: Addison-Wesley, 1995.

Ginsburg, William L. *Victims' Rights: A Complete Guide to Crime Victim Compensation.* Clearwater, FL: Sphinx Pub., 1994.

Pillegi, Nicholas. *Wiseguy: Life in a Mafia Family.* New York, NY: Simon & Schuster, 1985.

Snider, Robert M. "Coming Soon to a Theater Near You: 'Son of Sam' Laws Take Aim at Criminals' Literary Proceeds, But They Don't Always Hit the Target," *California Lawyer,* Vol. 7, no. 4 (April 1987).

Stark, James. *The Rights of Crime Victims.* New York, NY: Bantam Books, 1985.

INDEX

LANDMARK DECISIONS OF THE UNITED STATES SUPREME COURT

SCHOOL DESEGREGATION

OBSCENITY

SCHOOL PRAYER

FAIR TRIALS

SEXUAL PRIVACY

CENSORSHIP

ABORTION

AFFIRMATIVE ACTION

BOOK BANNING

FLAG BURNING

MAUREEN HARRISON & STEVE GILBERT
EDITORS

Also Available From Excellent Books

LANDMARK DECISIONS OF THE UNITED STATES SUPREME COURT II

SLAVERY

WOMEN'S SUFFRAGE

JAPANESE AMERICAN CONCENTRATION CAMPS

BIBLE READING IN THE PUBLIC SCHOOLS

THE BOOK BANNED IN BOSTON

RIGHTS OF THE ACCUSED

THE DEATH PENALTY

HOMOSEXUALITY

OFFENSIVE SPEECH

THE RIGHT TO DIE

MAUREEN HARRISON & STEVE GILBERT
EDITORS

Also Available From Excellent Books

LANDMARK DECISIONS OF THE UNITED STATES SUPREME COURT III

EXECUTIVE PRIVILEGE

CLEAR AND PRESENT DANGER

FORCED STERILIZATION

MOB JUSTICE

PLEDGE OF ALLEGIANCE

ILLEGAL SEARCH & SEIZURE

INTERRACIAL MARRIAGE

MONKEY TRIALS

SEXUAL HARASSMENT

CHURCH AND STATE

MAUREEN HARRISON & STEVE GILBERT
EDITORS

Also Available From Excellent Books

LANDMARK DECISIONS OF THE UNITED STATES SUPREME COURT IV

FEDERAL SUPREMACY

THE TRAIL OF TEARS

LINCOLN'S SUSPENSION OF HABEAS CORPUS

SEPARATE BUT EQUAL

TRUST BUSTING

CHILD LABOR

THE ATOMIC SPIES

LIBEL

CONSCIENTIOUS OBJECTION

HATE CRIMES

MAUREEN HARRISON & STEVE GILBERT
EDITORS

EXCELLENT BOOKS ORDER FORM

(Please xerox this form so it will be available to other readers.)

Please send

Copy(ies)

_____ of LANDMARK DECISIONS @ $14.95 each
_____ of LANDMARK DECISIONS II @ $15.95 each
_____ of LANDMARK DECISIONS III @ $15.95 each
_____ of LANDMARK DECISIONS IV @ $15.95 each
_____ of LANDMARK DECISIONS V @ $16.95 each
_____ of ABORTION DECISIONS: THE 1970's @ $15.95 each
_____ of ABORTION DECISIONS: THE 1980's @ $15.95 each
_____ of ABORTION DECISIONS: THE 1990's @ $15.95 each
_____ of CIVIL RIGHTS DECISIONS: 19th CENTURY @ $16.95 ea.
_____ of CIVIL RIGHTS DECISIONS: 20th CENTURY @ $16.95 ea.
_____ of ABRAHAM LINCOLN: WORD FOR WORD @ $19.95 each
_____ of THOMAS JEFFERSON: WORD FOR WORD @ $19.95 each
_____ of JOHN F. KENNEDY: WORD FOR WORD @ $19.95 each
_____ of THE ADA HANDBOOK @ $15.95 each

Name:_____

Address:_____

City:_____ **State:** _____ **Zip:** _____

Add $1 per book for shipping and handling
California residents add sales tax

OUR GUARANTEE: Any Excellent Book may be returned at any time for any reason and a full refund will be made.

Mail your check or money order to: Excellent Books,
Post Office Box 927105, San Diego, California 92192-7105
or call/fax (619) 457-4895